Bitter Truth

Bitter Truth

My Story of Bitterness, Grace, and Repentance

Linda R. Graf

Cross to Crown Ministries
Colorado Springs

Linda R. Graf, *Bitter Truth*

Copyright © 2014 by Linda R. Graf

Published by Cross to Crown Ministries
5210 Centennial Blvd
Colorado Springs, CO 80919
www.crosstocrown.org

Cover design by Daniel Davidson, Colorado Springs, CO
www.sadmonkeydesign.com

Back cover photo by Mandy Egolf, MandyMary
Photography www.mandymary.com

Printed in the United States of America

ISBN: 978-0-9851187-4-7

To my dear friends Bob and LeAnne:

Thank you for grace. I will always be grateful for how God worked through you.

Contents

Thanks...

A big thanks to Teren, Anne, Beth, Karri, Tracy, Alicia, Pam, Krista, and Sarah for reading the manuscript, giving feed-back, and tons of encouragement. I am also grateful for the invaluable support of my wonderful husband Dave. I am truly blessed to have such friends.

Prologue

My life became one of walking on eggshells, not knowing what I had done to set Linda off, and too afraid to
say or do much for fear of upsetting her. I don't want to
paint an inaccurate picture, she has never been a sweet
little cream-puff that I could walk all over, but she was
becoming entirely unreasonable in the things that would
make her hurt or angry. I also sensed profound sadness underneath the mask of normalcy that she would
sometimes put on. It's an incredibly lonely, heart-aching
experience to have your wife constantly upset with you.
It's even more heart-wrenching when you truly love her
and feel like you're the biggest reason why her life is
miserable.

~ David Graf

1

Why Am I Writing About Bitterness?

Because it almost got me.

Because I once needed a book like this.

Because I was once deeply entangled in it and couldn't see it. I didn't understand the problem was *my* sin. I thought it was everyone else's fault. Bitterness almost cost me my job, my church home, and many of my friends. It deeply affected my marriage and the relationship with my parents. It made me angry and miserable. Now that I understand it, I see it everywhere, but back then, in the midst of it, I was confused. I didn't know what was wrong or what to do.

When a godly friend said, "You are bitter, sister, you've got to let it go," I replied, "I probably am and I probably should, but how? What is it exactly? What do I do about it? Let it go? What does that look like?" I was dumbfounded. I wondered if it was really true. How does one define or identify bitterness? How could I change?

Don't misunderstand me, I know what the Bible teaches. I was raised in the church and graduated from a Christian college. I've done countless Bibles studies and heard many good sermons and lots of solid teaching. I've read the Bible through many times. I would rate my knowledge of Scripture as above average. Yet even with all of this understanding, I didn't recognize this most basic of sins and what it was doing to me.

So I went on a quest. I read the Bible with a focused eye and searched for Christian books about anger and bitterness. I talked to people and observed their behavior. Mostly, I asked God to give me insight and wisdom. He was faithful and showed me my sin, and then He gave me the power to repent and change. He's certainly not finished yet, and I'm still tempted to bitterness at times, but He has changed me so much that I just cannot help but tell others about it.

Maybe you'll see it in yourself, too, as you read.

That's why I am writing my story. I hope to define exactly what bitterness is, describe what it looks like, illustrate its effects, and prescribe how to wipe it out. For me, I know it will be a lifelong struggle. But God is gracious and forgiving. He knows we are weak and helps us when we ask. He has worked mightily already. I've come so far, but still have a ways to go. I've experienced reconciliation, renewed love, and renewed joy. That is what I wish for you, if this is your struggle.

I firmly believe that bitterness is one of the most beguiling of sins. We can easily delude ourselves into thinking it's not a problem, it's not so bad, or it's not our fault. *After all, there are so many sins out there that are much worse.* Our eyes are easily diverted from our own failings. And it's easy to feel sorry for ourselves. We look at others and see that their lives are so much happier, things are much easier for them than for us, and we feel entitled to a little self-pity. This goes hand-in-hand with our entitlement culture exhorting us to look out for Number One, that *we* have the right to be happy and get what *we* want.

But we don't have to succumb to society and sin. In this book, I hope to make it easier, offering a battle plan of sorts, for those engaged in the same fight. If you struggle with bitterness, remember—God is more powerful than even the deepest, most habitual, and firmly rooted sin. Nothing is impossible with Him! In John 16:33, Jesus said, "I have told you these things, so that in me you may have peace. In this world you will have trouble. But take heart! I have overcome the world" (NIV). Through His power, we can overcome the sin of this world and its entanglements, even bitterness.

2

Getting and Staying Bitter in Five Easy Steps

I'm going to give you a page from my *Personal Bitterness Handbook*. Consider it helpful advice from a bitterness expert.

1. Pick someone to become bitter against. (Note: You can have more than one person, but it's extra work and not recommended for beginners. Go slowly at first.) It should be someone you interact with regularly, preferably someone close to you. Good suggestions include your spouse, a parent or sibling, your boss, a co-worker, a neighbor or close friend. This is usually the easiest part. We will call this person your "Pylon" (pile-on, get it?).

2. Start building your pile. Just keep track of every offense, no matter how small. It's like building a compost heap in your backyard. Slow and steady builds a big pile! Decide 'what is true' about your Pylon, especially how they feel about you. Then take everything they say and do and place it under one of these headings:

- They don't like or love me.

- They don't respect me.

- They don't appreciate or notice me.

- They are out to get me.

- They think I'm fat.

Sometimes it's difficult to do this. You must twist their words or actions to fit one of these headings, but be creative and persistent. You can do it!

3. Become an expert pile-builder. As your pile grows, you must actively maintain it. Observe your Pylon. How do they treat others? (No doubt better than they treat you!) Blame the Pylon for your pile. Look for ways to add to and stir up your pile. Rehearse every offensive thing they say or do. Ignore any kindness the Pylon may commit. Feel sorry for yourself. A lot. Sit and look at your pile and think, "Poor me, this is so unfair. That Pylon gets away with so much. Someone should know how poorly I am treated, how stinky this pile is." As you become proficient at this, your Pylon may even make it easy for you! They may casually walk by and toss a rotten banana peel onto your pile. If that happens, be sure to take a picture of it. Enlarge it to poster size and add the caption: "See? I have this pile because they built it for me!" Plaster these posters all over your house. And don't forget to feel sorry for yourself.

4. Refute any attempt at apology or reconciliation. This rarely happens, but sometimes your Pylon may actually realize they've done wrong to you and try to apologize. Surely they have some ulterior motive or just want to look good. You must hold fast! Stand firm on top of your pile! You can always find fault with an apology. Perhaps they didn't say it quite right or use the correct words. Maybe they didn't apologize with enough feeling (did they even cry?). Perhaps they were coerced by someone else or were concerned about their image. Maybe you *just know* they didn't mean it. All of these are good reasons to disregard said apology.

If you are tempted to forgive the Pylon, review your pile and think about all the other things in the pile that they *haven't* apologized for. If necessary, be polite and tell them it's okay, just to smooth things over, but don't mean it. Don't let your beautiful pile disappear!

5. Share with others, hide from God. Tell others about your Pylon and about your pile. Be careful to phrase it delicately so you don't appear malicious or bitter. Make it sound like a prayer request or asking for advice regarding the Pylon. If someone accuses you of bitterness or confronts you with wrongdoing, go on the attack. Point out areas where *they* are weak, and they don't really know the whole story anyway! Whatever you do, don't tell God about your pile. Keep it hidden from Him and well-covered, especially when you go to church. Never examine your own heart or consider that you may be in any way to blame in this relationship with your Pylon.

If you do all these things well, you will grow, simmer, and ferment a nice big pile. It will start to stink so pungently that it will permeate not only your backyard, but your entire house as well. You may even give some of it away. Go ahead, spread it to others. After all, we're taught that sharing is a good thing. When people knock on your door, they will know (smell) immediately that you are a successful 'pile-builder' and will be awed and amazed. Congratulations!

The righteous hate what is false, but the wicked make themselves a stench and bring shame on themselves. (Proverbs 13:5 NIV)

PART I

My Story

3

Deep Roots

Looking back, I can see now that I started building piles against my parents very early in life. It became evident when I was a young newlywed. Although I wouldn't have known to call it bitterness at that time, I was angry and hurt, and I definitely wanted them to feel it.

I got married the year I graduated from college, as did many of my friends. But my experience leading up to the big day seemed considerably lacking in comparison to theirs: brides were pampered and consulted about everything they wanted, relatives traveled long distances to attend, grandparents gave family heirlooms as cherished gifts, parents were emotional, sad even, yet excited for their daughter.

My parents and I argued about almost everything. The food, the flowers, and especially the wedding photography were all points of contention. I was accused of wanting too much, being too extravagant, spending too much money.

I was especially upset about my wedding pictures. Rather than hire a professional photographer to create a nice wedding album, they wanted a family member to take snapshots. It would save money, and he wanted to bless us in this way. I protested vigorously, but my arguments were ignored. The photos were a complete disaster, and it was all their fault. They had insisted on *their* way, and now there was no going back, no redoing that special day.

I could not hold back my deep disappointment. I had to tell them about my wedding frustrations. But as I did, what came out went way beyond the photo album. Once those floodgates were opened, a torrent of emotion was released. I began to pound them with years of bitter feelings and hurt. I was consumed with self-pity: They had never loved me like they should have. They had never encouraged me. They always pointed out every little flaw and failure. They didn't care about my feelings, only about appearances and what their friends would think. The wedding just illustrated what had been true all along—while other fathers wept as they brought their daughters down the aisle, mine was relieved to get me off his hands. I imagined him exclaiming, "Finally! We are done with her!"

Their response? They defended themselves. They said the whole thing came off wonderfully. They accused me of being too sensitive and selfish since, after all, they had paid for it. And they had paid for my entire college education, and music lessons before that, and summer camps, and private schools, and just about anything else I had ever wanted or needed. Plus, we took great vacations every summer, they were generous at birthdays and Christmas, Mom stayed at home with us, we were raised in the church, we went out to eat often. What more did I need?

So I told them.

And they defended themselves again, saying they had done what they thought was right, that my childhood was better than theirs had been, and that they hadn't *tried* to be evil, neglectful parents. Then they reminded me of what a rebellious handful I had been. For example, the party I threw when I was sixteen which resulted in the police being called. They said I was profoundly selfish and ungrateful for all that they had done for me.

We argued like this for months. We were all miserable.

Finally, I realized it was futile. I would never convince them that they were at fault. We would never agree about what was true. This was only straining our relationship, so I dropped it. I stopped arguing. I stopped bringing up the past. I still cried from time to time over my wedding pictures, but there was nothing that could be done about it.

FEELING ABANDONED
(EVEN IF I'M THE ONE WHO LEFT)

Fast forward a few years later. My husband and I moved across the country, far away from my parents. We saw them and spoke to them less often, and when we did, I tried to keep our interactions pleasant. But then came the birth of my first child, and bitterness reared its ugly head again.

I was the perfect picture of an inept new mother. I had not been around babies much in my growing-up years, and

I felt completely out of my element. I desperately wanted help from my mother, but she was taking care of her elderly mother and didn't feel that she could be away for even a short time. My father and sister came instead. I was glad for their company, but they weren't exactly the hands-on help I wanted and needed.

During their visit, my husband had knee surgery and became terribly sick from the anesthesia. Then, to complicate an already tenuous situation, my baby developed a life-threatening condition which required immediate surgery. I felt like the world was crashing down around me, *and I was without my mother.* I was drowning in fear and self-pity and felt like no one cared. I was completely alone.

But that's not a fair assessment. (Although I couldn't see it then, I now realize that this is what bitterness does, it remembers only what it chooses to, and it puts a negative spin on those events.) Our wonderful church family did come alongside us during this time. A dear friend Mary, my surrogate mother really, was a tremendous help. Other families sent meals, flowers, and encouraging words. I was by no means alone or abandoned. Yet all I could think about was that my own mother was not there when I really needed her.

And let's not forget that my father *was* there. He sat with me in the doctor's waiting room while my sick baby lay limp in my arms. He knew that I was about five seconds away from total panic, so he did the only thing he could think of. He started telling me stories about some of our relatives and their weird medical problems. Bizarre, gross stories! At one point I remember saying to him, *"What in the world are you telling me?"* He was doing his best to distract me and get my mind off the desperation I felt. And it worked. I held it together emotionally while the doctor made a quick diagnosis and we were rushed to the hospital.

But this did nothing to change the picture in my mind of how neglectful and uncaring my parents were. As my kids grew up, I grew increasingly bitter at their lack of interest and involvement as grandparents. They live far away, which made it difficult to

I now realize that this is what bitterness does, it remembers only what it chooses to, and it puts a negative spin on those events.

build relationships, but it seemed to me more a matter of priority than distance. I was deeply saddened and angered that my kids were growing up without knowing or feeling love from their maternal grandparents.

The roots of bitterness were being cemented into my heart.

4

First Roots

Like I said, I didn't realize my bitterness until I was an adult, but it's clear to me now that the weed began to sprout when I was just a child. Let's back up to the beginning.

A LITTLE BACKGROUND

I grew up in a blended family. By that I mean both of my parents were married previously and had each lost their spouses to death. My dad met Cathy through their church when I was four years old. (My older sister Dianne was nineteen and away at college. She never really became part of the new family, although she got along well with Cathy.) With my new mother came two new brothers, Andrew and David, who were five and seven.

Ray and Cathy were thrilled with each other. They took romantic getaways a couple of times a year. They were active in church and had many good friends. They sang in the choir, participated in prayer meetings, and Ray served on the deacon board. Cathy volunteered in various children's ministries and was active for years with Christian Women's Clubs. Theirs was a happy life. It still is, even after more than 45 years. I have never heard them fight or even strongly argue. Dad always treats Mom like the queen. Whatever she wants, or even hints at, he is happy to do. And she has always respected him, spoken well of him, and appreciated him.

RULES, RULES, RULES

They were thrilled with each other, but were less thrilled to have three rambunctious children in the household. They established a host of rules to regulate our lives, rules about *everything*: shoes, coats, snacks, bedtime, TV, playing outside. Most of the rules made sense, but they were all set in stone, no exceptions, no deviations. One time, a babysitter let us stay up thirty minutes past our bedtime; we never had her again. We only ate at the kitchen table, and there was no eating between meals except for one snack when we got home from school—seated at the table. (In my teen years, some of my wild rebellion was bringing a bag of pretzels into my room to eat while working on homework.) We had rules about modesty, cleanliness, and chores. Punishment was consistent: if you spilled food on the floor, you were fined a portion of your allowance. Everything was regulated.

The hardest rules for me to follow were the ones that stifled us socially. No children were allowed in our house, and we did not go into other kids' homes. This wasn't too hard on my brothers who were mostly riding bikes, hiking through the woods, or playing kickball or football in the backyard, but it was hard on me since the girls in my neighborhood wanted to play Barbies or games which were all inside. So I either hung out with the boys or stayed to myself. We were also not allowed to have birthday parties with friends. It didn't bother me until I got invited to a few parties and saw what fun it was to have a big deal made of your special day. But those invitations were rare because I never had my own party (or so I assumed). Besides, I was just odd. We had so many rules in our family that other kids thought we were weird. I remember reciting our litany of regulations to a neighbor girl while she looked at me as if I had two heads. I didn't really know how to interact with other girls and had very few friends.

The most difficult rule for my brothers was that Saturday was always a work day. The girls did inside work, the boys did outside work. We lived at the very edge of our subdivision, with a large yard backing up to an extensive wooded area, acres and acres that you could get lost in for days. This meant endless yardwork: mowing, raking, trimming bushes and trees, and weeding gardens. I would do my inside chores and be done. The boys, however, would never be done. They would do the jobs Dad had ordered, and then he would come up with something else for them because he believed they should learn to do hard work. "Life is not about playing," he would say, "it's about learning to work." And Dad is a hard worker. He was out there all day on Saturdays himself. The neighborhood kids would come by and ask, "When will you be done? When can you play?" Andrew and David would beg for reprieve, but Dad always said no because he wanted to keep them busy all day. Almost every Saturday was filled with arguing and anger. The boys grew to resent Dad for these rules and to resent me because I had more free time than they did on weekends.

And I resented them for resenting me.

LIVING WITH A BULLY

My parents often went out with their friends which meant that when we were younger we had babysitters at least twice each week. This was actually a good thing for me because I loved getting the attention of a teenage girl, one of whom even led me to Christ while my parents were out to dinner. However, when my older brother David turned twelve, Mom and Dad decided they didn't need babysitters anymore because David was old enough to be in charge. (I was nine, Andrew was ten.) The next several years were really rough. Mom and Dad got involved in more things at church and started going to dinner with their friends every Saturday night as well. They left us alone in the evenings five times a week, and on Sunday nights they would have their friends over after evening church services.

David is artistic and melancholy. He has always been an introvert like his mother. Andrew is outgoing and charismatic like his father was, a born leader. He also became quite a bully, not just with us, but with the neighborhood kids as well. David may have been *officially* in charge when Mom and Dad were gone, but Andrew was really the one in control. He made life miserable. Sometimes, he would terrorize both David and me, other times the boys would join forces to torment me. Andrew never abused me physically, but he often threatened to punch me out, and I knew he could do it if I didn't go along with his plans. This situation continued for four or five years.

If we complained to our parents, David was told, "You're older and bigger. Don't let him push you around. Don't be a sissy," and I was told, "Just ignore him. Stay away from him. You're too sensitive." When we asked them to stay home more because we didn't want to be left alone with Andrew, Dad would say, "Your mother is home every single day with you. She deserves a little fun. You're being selfish." I think they really didn't understand how bad it was. I still remember the dread I felt as evening approached and it was time for Mom and Dad to go out.

Every interaction with my brothers turned into a quarrel. I was constantly mocked and ridiculed. I knew that no one would come to my defense, so I either had to fight back or hide. I learned to be happy alone in my room with my books and music and tried to avoid my brothers as much as possible.

SCHOOL DAYS, SCHOOL DAYS

During this time we were enrolled in a private Christian school that was part of a church in town. It was small (less than fifty students), and there were few girls around my age. Once a girlfriend invited me to her house, and my parents let me go. What I saw there shocked me. She and her siblings laid on the couch or floor eating snacks and watching TV. After school! (I'm sure in my awkwardness I informed them that I was not allowed to eat between meals, or eat on the couch, or watch TV after school, et cetera, et cetera.) Also shocking was the *friendly* banter between her and her siblings. They teased and argued, but everyone seemed to actually like each other. I had never seen such behavior in a family.

The Christian school was very strict. Andrew especially hated its rigidity and was often in trouble. After three years, he was expelled, so we all went back to public school.

I entered 8th grade totally clueless about how to dress or behave. I didn't have the right jeans, my body didn't have the right curves, I couldn't wear makeup, and I had no idea how to make friends. One popular girl quickly befriended me as the "new girl," but she soon realized that I was awkward and hopeless and wouldn't fit into her group. She stopped talking to me and pretended I didn't exist. I resented her the rest of my high school years, taking every opportunity to speak ill of her.

The summer I turned fourteen, Andrew was fifteen, and he started running away. He would go into the woods for days at a time and not come home. When he did come around, there would be a big fight. Dad would demand that Andrew obey the rules of the house. Andrew would say "Your rules stink, and I'm not going to follow them." Then he would disappear again. Finally, there was a big showdown involving broken glass, injury, the police, and social services. Everyone agreed that Andrew could no longer live in our house. He went to stay with an uncle who lived about forty-five minutes away. He never lived at home again.

My mother was broken-hearted over this. I was so happy I couldn't stand it, like I had been given a whole new lease on life. David and I didn't get along, but I wasn't afraid of him. He didn't bully me like Andrew had. We mostly just left each other alone. I was more relaxed and started making some friends and trying new things. I felt like a black cloud had been lifted. Yet, I was still convinced that my weird family and our strict rules prevented me from having any kind of a normal life.

SWEET BITTER SIXTEEN

My First Job. The summer I turned sixteen, I got a job at the brand new McDonald's that had opened in our town. I was a diligent employee, advancing to the front register after only a few months. My friend Susan lived nearby, and one summer day she rode her bike over to wait for me to get off work. It was the middle of the afternoon, and the restaurant was completely empty. We were wiping down machines and looking for ways to keep busy. She came in, ordered french fries and a soda, and then proceeded to pay me entirely with pennies. She laughed while I painstakingly counted them. We stood and chatted until the fries were ready. As I handed them to her, I said, "I think I deserve some fries for all my hard work counting pennies," and took two from her bag. We stood there a few minutes longer until my manager came out and said that I could go home. This was good news to us. Susan went to wait outside, and I went to get my things. As I moved to the back, my manager said, "You're leaving because you're fired. I saw you eat those french fries. Taking a customer's food is a serious offense!" I was stunned. I didn't know what to say. I just grabbed my stuff and left. We went to Susan's house, and I remember lying on her floor curled up in a ball. I was absolutely convinced at that point that I was a complete failure. I knew I would never amount to anything in life. I had just been fired from my first job. Who would ever hire me again to do anything? How could I ever expect to succeed at anything on any level?

My father told me I should go back to McDonald's and talk to the manager. I should apologize and ask for a second chance. I saw that as an invitation to further humiliation, and I just couldn't do it. In fact, it was years before I felt comfortable going into that McDonald's again.

My First Boyfriend. Phil asked me to a dance my junior year of high school. We started dating after that. Our interest in each other was fairly mild. I was just excited that someone liked me enough to make an effort.

One night, Phil told me that after he got off work he would swing by my house and we'd go out for ice cream. I waited by my front door for several hours, but he never showed. I had been officially stood up! I was furious. The next day at school when I confronted him, he laughed and shrugged it off as unimportant. It was not unimportant to me, I felt humiliated. After this, I was not kind to him. He needed to understand what he had done. He needed to be punished. I was sarcastic and critical and unpleasant. After a few weeks of this, he broke up with me (surprise!). He was actually pretty nice about it, but I was devastated — not because I had strong feelings for Phil, but because I knew it had been all my own fault. I had driven him away with my behavior, but I couldn't seem to help it. What was wrong with me?

My First Party. Mom and Dad took a vacation to Bermuda that May, and they decided that David and I would be fine on our own for a week. Since I had just gotten my driver's license, they made it clear that they were not leaving me keys. I was not to drive while they were gone. They also gave strict instructions not to have anybody in the house.

But I had a plan.

On Monday morning, after my brother left for classes, I wrote several excuse notes for my friends (for their "doctor" or "dentist" appointments) and picked them up from school at various intervals during the morning in my parents' van. (I had secretly made copies of the keys before they left.) It was all carefully spaced out so the teachers wouldn't figure out that they were skipping school together. I had a neighbor buy a case of beer, and *we had a party.*

Lots of planning and coordination had gone into this affair, and for a while it was great fun. But then my friend Timmy, who had had too much to drink, decided to take my parents' van on a joyride through the neighborhood. He whipped recklessly around residential streets at high speed. There were little children playing outside, and a concerned mom called the police. Meanwhile, we were playing my brother's stereo so loud that the speakers started smoking and blew up. (My hair almost caught fire.) They caught Timmy before he could hurt anyone, and he spent the night in jail. Since my parents were out of the country, the police called my brother-in-law. But they made an appointment to talk to my parents when they got back. When that moment arrived, it was truly dramatic. They were terribly shocked.

Mom cried. They said, "We will never trust you again." I was grounded indefinitely.

It ended up being for the rest of that year. For seven or eight months, I went to school and to church and to piano lessons and nowhere else. I didn't talk on the phone. I didn't drive the car. I didn't go to friends' houses. I didn't do anything fun. Complete restriction. But at school, I was a hero – my popularity increased dramatically.

I was not sorry at all. I may have said I was sorry, but I had absolutely no remorse for what I had done. I was now famous! People now knew I was *that girl who had the party and the police came*. It was the turning point in my social life.

After I was freed from my punishment, I redoubled my efforts to deceive my parents. I snuck around. I lied to them. If they didn't trust me, why should I be trustworthy? I wanted to have fun and go to parties and date. I knew it was wrong. I knew what the Bible says about lying and disobeying your parents, but I felt like I had no other options. They forced me into it. If they hadn't been so strict, I wouldn't be so bad. My sins were justified. I told myself, "God will understand, and I'll straighten out later."

5

My Bitter Worldview

Growing up in that environment produced long-lasting problems and temptations. I learned to believe lies about myself that tainted every aspect of my life. They formed the lens through which I saw the world, or rather, through which I believed the world saw me.

Belief 1—No one really likes you or is interested in you. You're a nuisance. No one in my family liked having me around. My brothers were out to get me, and my parents were disinterested and critical. I didn't have many friends. I was better off keeping to myself because if someone did get to know me, they would eventually find out I'm awkward and hopeless and then reject me.

Because of this belief, I desperately wanted to be liked and accepted throughout my teen years. I went along with the crowd so that I would fit in, which led to much sinful behavior. Even today, I often try too hard to be liked. I seek acceptance by being funny. Sometimes my humor is at someone else's expense. I put others down so I will look good by comparison. Sometimes, in my attempt to make a story funny, I embellish to the point of lying. Many temptations accompany the desire to be liked.

This lie also causes me to fear meeting new people. *Why would they want to meet me?* I reason, *of course they won't like me.* When someone new comes to our church, I let others greet them, people who are likable and worthy of getting to know.

More significantly, I have a hard time believing that my heavenly Father delights in me as His beloved daughter. This lie can be a severe spiritual handicap.

Belief 2—No one will come to your defense. You have to fight your own battles. Get them before they get you. I learned the *fight or flight* mode because of my brothers. I couldn't depend on anyone to come to my defense. I had to be tough.

This lie creates a wary defensiveness and distrust. I am ready to fight back at a moment's notice, especially with a sharp, sarcastic tongue that could shred anyone. The number of harsh things I have said is staggering. And my self-defense is usually justified by self-pity, a regular temptation that accompanies this belief.

Belief 3—You are untrustworthy. You always do the wrong thing. You're always "bad." Of course, there was the big party, but I couldn't even hold down a job at McDonald's. And what did all the strict house rules mean but,

"If *you* have snacks in the living room, you will inevitably ruin our nice furniture or carpet." My mother didn't teach me to cook or do laundry because she didn't want me messing up her kitchen or tampering with her washing machine.

Like *Belief 1*, this comes into play when I meet new people. I fear saying something wrong and offending them, ruining any chance of friendship. Or when my job requires me to have a tough conversation with someone, I am terrified because, of course, I will not do it right and will probably cause serious fallout. Or if you tell me a secret, I get nervous because I might forget and tell everyone. Or when given the opportunity to share the gospel, I am convinced I will spew heresy within the first sentence and totally misrepresent God's grace. The greatest result of believing this lie is fear.

Belief 4—Even when you do well, it's never quite good enough. I was becoming a proficient pianist, but after a concert or a special performance, I received faint praise mixed with criticism because my parents didn't want me to get a "big head." And even though I graduated high school with honors, what was remembered is that I almost failed one science class. My family was all too happy to bring up the past and my many failures. The message I heard was, "Even your best efforts aren't enough for you to be accepted and loved."

The temptation here is to just give up the pursuit of holiness. *Why should I try to follow the rules? I'm not going to be accepted either way so I may as well have some fun. Besides, the Bible says that none of our righteous acts count for salvation. We* are saved only by God's grace through faith. *If my righteousness does nothing for my relationship with God, and if I'm never going to be good enough for people down here, what's the point of trying?* So I considered myself "saved" but on the lowest rung of Christians in God's eyes (more self-pity). He had to save me because I believed the gospel, but there was little hope of my becoming like Jesus. This lie caused me to distort the gospel and believe that I was incapable of righteous living.

Belief 5—There is no forgiveness for you. My parents reminded me of "the party" for years. Other past offenses would be routinely brought up just to prove a point in the current argument. When my father suggested I apologize to the manager at McDonald's and ask for my job back, I just knew there was no way that would happen. No one was going to forget what I did and give me another chance.

Believing this lie provokes me to be judgmental and unforgiving toward others. If no one will cut me any slack, why should I do it for others? If it's *one strike and you're out* for me, it should be for you, too. When I don't believe that anyone shows grace to me (especially God), I struggle greatly to show grace to others.

Bitterness creates a false view of God, the world, and you.

THERE IS HOPE

I still fight these deep-seated lies. When thinking soberly, I know they aren't true, but too often they *feel* true, which usually trumps the thinking. I have to battle constantly and ask Jesus to transform my feelings or else run the risk of being a prime candidate for bitterness.

But here is the good news—Jesus *does* help. He does bring truth and transformation. So if you see any of these beliefs in yourself, please hear me when I say there is hope for you no matter your background or personality or past sins.

6

Full-Grown Weeds

My bitterness had reached full bloom. Every relationship held the potential for anger and resentment. I became indignant at several bosses for not promoting me or giving me greater opportunities. I held grudges against friends and pushed them away. And I have certainly struggled with bitterness toward my husband. After all, who is closer than your spouse? Who has more opportunity to irritate and disappoint you?

Then there's my current job situation. I work for a godly Christian man. As of this writing, we have well over a decade of history together. I'm sorry to say that many of those years I wasted in bitterness toward him. Is it because he's a bad guy? On the contrary, he is well-loved by many. He has devoted his life and career to building up the church and spreading the gospel. He has also shown me more grace and forgiveness than most people would, given the circumstances.

I work in my church and my boss is the pastor. His name is

Doug. Fifteen years ago, when he joined the staff, he inherited the responsibility for me and my ministry. Doug is a gifted musician as well as a pastor, and since I'm in charge of the music ministry our then senior pastor decided, quite logically, to make him my supervisor. I liked Doug immediately and anticipated a wonderful working relationship. We have many things in common including taste in music and sense of humor. We agree on most things relating to the church and ministry. But our personalities are vastly different.

At first, I was frustrated by his style of administration. I felt overlooked and found myself begging for his time and attention. Then I began to feel unappreciated and ignored because he didn't give me the respect or affirmation I desired. He didn't respond to me the way I believed a good boss or a good pastor should. So I became angry. When he didn't react to my anger the way I thought he would (he was very rational and calm), I became even angrier. It came out in unkind and ungodly ways (I berated and accused him and cried a lot). Usually he responded with a few carefully chosen words of truth, which only added fuel to my fire. Afterwards I would feel ashamed and sorry for my outburst, and I would apologize, which he always graciously accepted. This cycle continued for years. We would get along for a few months, then my hurt and anger would build until it got to the breaking point. Then another blowup, making an apology necessary *again*.

You may think we should have just given up on the relationship. After all, why put ourselves through this? Why not just accept that we cannot get along? Maybe Doug should just fire me or I should leave and go somewhere else. But there were good times, too. I mentioned earlier that we have lots in common. We would often get laughing together during our meetings, disturbing everyone else in the office. One Christmas, after consulting my husband, Doug gave me an amazing and unexpected gift just to show his care and appreciation. And my husband and I painted and redecorated his office to celebrate his election to be our senior pastor. I would sometimes make his favorite dessert. It wasn't all strife and conflict. Yet our relationship continued to deteriorate.

For a long time, I thought it was hopeless. I loved my church and my job, but I couldn't consistently get along with my boss. What made it harder to bear was that there were few people I could share my frustrations with. I know what the Bible teaches about spreading gossip. It's a terrible, destructive sin. I experienced a church split during my childhood and realized that bad-mouthing the pastor could be the first step in breaking unity and promoting dissension. What if our church split apart because I told everyone how awful Doug was? I quaked in my boots at the thought of being responsible for such an appalling outcome. I was doomed to suffer in silence.

During this time, when our relationship was at its worst, we were in the process of building a new church facility. It was a big undertaking and God performed many miracles to bring it about. I was excited to help with the decorating and furnishing team. But the purchase I was most anxiously anticipating was a gorgeous baby grand piano. A generous family donated money, and I got to pick out the exact model I wanted. It was in storage, awaiting completion of our building. I could hardly stand the wait.

But then came *the day*. Doug and I had a particularly bad argument. He was tired of my accusations and complaints, and this time he let me have it (very calmly and rationally, of course). He recounted some unkind things I had said to him in front of the whole music team before the worship service the previous Sunday. He told me I was bitter against him and that it had to stop.

It would stop alright. I drove away from the church that day in tears, vowing never to return. I couldn't continue on, enough was enough. I had reached the absolute breaking point. I was done!

But then I remembered…*the piano was being delivered the next day!* I was in torment. How could I leave *now* after I had waited so long for my beautiful piano?

I would stay for one more day.

PART II

Bitterness—What Is It?

7

Bitterness Defined

I will tell the rest of my story with Doug as we go. (It turns out very well. God is gracious!) But now I want to move toward a definition of bitterness. This section is the answer to the heartfelt cry I once asked, "What exactly *is* bitterness? Someone please explain it to me!" Let's start with the standard dictionary definitions of *bitter*.

DEFINITIONS

adjective
>1 *having a sharp, pungent taste or smell; not sweet.*
>2 *angry, hurt, or resentful because of one's bad experiences or a sense of unjust treatment.*
>3 *painful or unpleasant to accept or contemplate.*
>4 *intensely cold.*

noun
>1 *Brit. beer that is strongly flavored with hops and has a bitter taste.*

2 liquor that is flavored with the sharp pungent taste of plant extracts and is used as an additive in cocktails or as a medicinal substance to promote appetite or digestion.

ORIGIN Old English *biter*, of Germanic origin; related to Dutch and German *bitter*, and probably to *bite*.

New Oxford American Dictionary

Bitterness is like drinking poison and hoping your enemy will die.

Notice that every possible way this word is used is negative: *bitter taste, bitter anguish, bad experiences, biting words*. There is nothing desirable or lovely about any of its possible uses. We would not want to be the recipient of a "bitter" anything. You can see why selfish anger, resentment, and spite have come to be called *bitter*-ness.

In Jerry Bridges' excellent book *Respectable Sins*, he has a chapter entitled "The Weeds of Anger" where he defines bitterness as "resentment that has grown into a feeling of ongoing animosity. Whereas resentment may dissipate over time, bitterness continues to grow and fester, developing an even higher degree of ill-will. It is usually the long-term reaction to real or perceived wrong when the initial anger is not dealt with" (p. 130).

We begin with anger. If the anger lingers, it grows into resentment. After resentment, it hardens into bitterness and then can even proceed to outright hatred and violence.

Another way to describe bitterness is *a negative response to being wronged*, whether that wrong is real or imagined. It is holding a grudge or a living in a consistent state of unforgiveness.

Jim Wilson, in *How to Be Free From Bitterness,* writes, "Bitterness is based on sin that somehow relates to you. It is not concerned with how big the sin is; it is based upon how close it is" (p. 9).

Bitterness is the response to a close, personal offense. You are not bitter over people being persecuted in other parts of the world. You may be sad or angry about it, but it does not affect you personally. When an offense is 'close to home,' it elicits a very different response. We cry, "Hey! That's not fair! That's not right! They shouldn't have done or said that!" But they did do it and maybe they do it again and again. We can't believe they are getting away with it. We wonder why someone doesn't do something about this! We ask, "Where is justice? Why doesn't someone defend me? Why is there no payback? After all, I'm the innocent victim here. I deserve better treatment than this."

Do you see the point? You may feel sorrow or even outrage over injustices done in other parts of the world, but it is not the same as the resentment you experience when you feel wronged.

As we let our hearts marinate in this kind of thinking, we travel from anger to resentment to bitterness, subtly sliding into self-pity and the desire for revenge as well. We end up holding a grudge and living in a consistent state of unforgiveness until it finally comes out in sinful and destructive ways.

Let me offer my own picture of bitterness—it is anger (originating from a perceived offense) that grows around the heart like a root until it hardens and chokes out love, leaving nothing soft or warm inside.

If I am bitter toward you, I will not consider your side of the story or be willing to view things from your perspective. I will have no empathy for your feelings—I will show you no grace. I will be a harsh and unforgiving judge, quickly jumping to conclusions. I will stay busy collecting evidence which proves you are indeed the monster I've made you out to be. No allowance is made for possible misinterpretations or misunderstandings. I'm sure I know what you meant by what you said or did.

THINK OF ASPEN TREES

I live in Colorado where aspen trees abound. They bountifully cover the mountains with their distinctively white bark. In the fall, their leaves turn glorious shades of gold, shimmering and quaking in the breeze. Yet these stately, elegant trees have a dark side.

Aspens have extensive root systems that can grow up to 40 feet away from the parent tree. They typically grow in large clonal colonies derived from a single seedling and spread by means of root suckers—little seedlings that grow underground and then sprout up. And while an individual aspen tree can live for 40–150 years above ground, the root system of the colony can persist for thousands of years, sending up new trunks as the older ones die off above ground.[1] Aspens are difficult to destroy. They can even survive forest fires because the roots live below the heat of the blaze.

Here is one woman's sad story of struggling with aspens in her backyard:

My yard, I am excited to report, is host to four aspen trees. Or it seemed like four when I moved in. Upon closer examination of my yard, I discovered that I had more than four big aspen trees. I had about thirty. One problem was that most of these trees were of the short, barely noticeable variety. This was not a problem as much as where these aspen juniors seemed to be sprouting. Most of them were closer to the structure of the house than their taller, well-established and obviously wiser brethren. The short distance between these young trees and the house made me imagine a not-too-distant future where an out-of-control root system tears out my underground sprinklers and infiltrates the plumbing. With my deepest apologies to the National Arbor Foundation, I decided to remove some of these extra trees. It turns out that you can't just dig up an aspen tree, yank the roots out of the dirt and be done with it. I tried. Some of the baby aspen trees were as thin as a pencil and no more than six inches tall. Yet when I tried to pull them up, they resisted as if they were much, much larger. I was flabbergasted. Were these trees ganging up on me? They clearly outnumbered me. Perhaps they

1. The Pando (aka *The Trembling Giant*) in Utah is considered by some to be the oldest living organism on earth.

sensed my fear about the plumbing. I decided to do a little research. It is important to know what you are up against. In the dry regions of the western United States, the aspen tree sometimes uses a method of reproduction called 'cloning'. Aspen trees can share a root system – they can actually be attached to each other deep under the ground. This was my yard problem. Those baby trees that refused to be uprooted were part of a much larger life form.[2]

The aspen root system illustrates bitterness very well:

1. Old trees are easily replaced with new ones because the roots remain intact. The same is true with bitterness. I can start being bitter against my parents, and quickly transition to my husband, boss, or close friend. It can become a habit, my normal mode of reaction to others.

2. Aspen colonies grow quickly and become quite large (over 106 acres in one case). So it is with bitterness. It can dominate our life and take over our thoughts.

3. The aspen's sturdy roots seek out water sources and in the process can tear up sidewalks, infiltrate sewer systems, and crowd out other healthy vegetation in a yard. Bitterness wants to spread into every thought, every evaluation, and every conversation. As it does, it taints many relationships and can keep spiritual fruit from growing in a Christian's life.

2. This is taken from an essay called *Life in Colorado* by Maleesha K. Speer at www.aroundcolorado.com (which at publication appeared to be missing).

4. The best way to kill aspens is by *girdling*, a wounding process which cuts the flow of nutrients between the roots and the crown. Eliminating bitterness also requires painful incisions to the heart to sever the flow of anger and selfishness.

5. Aspen root systems are long-lived. Bitterness may be passed along from generation to generation. I may unconsciously teach my children to react bitterly through my bad example. And I may act bitterly toward them, which could provoke them to anger and resentment, repeating the same awful cycle.

6. Aspens can also become a tangled web as older roots weave together with roots of newer growth. The same is true with bitterness. If I respond poorly to an offense, my own anger may be so mixed in that it becomes a jumbled mess making it impossible to tell where it started or who is more at fault. Reconciliation becomes an arduous, prolonged process.

BITTERNESS IS SIN

Many people, myself included, excuse bitterness, saying, "I am only trying to make sure justice is served," or "I can't help it, they wronged me!" But we need to come to the realization that these reactions and justifications are sin.

The Bible says, "My dear brothers and sisters, take note of this: Everyone should be quick to listen, slow to speak and slow to become angry, because human anger does not produce the righteousness that God desires" (James 1:19-20 NIV). The thing we are to be "quick to listen" to is the gospel, the "word of truth" (James 1:18, 21). We are to take time to slowly formulate our speech so that it conforms to and aligns with God's message of grace. If, when we feel offended, we review the gospel, we will not quickly fly to anger because our minds will be focused less on ourselves and more on Him. We can't be stewing in anger and conforming to the gospel at the same time. This will lead us toward the righteous life God desires for us.

> *And do not bring sorrow to God's Holy Spirit by the way you live. Remember, he has identified you as his own, guaranteeing that you will be saved on the day of redemption. Get rid of all bitterness, rage, anger, harsh words, and slander, as well as all types of evil behavior. Instead, be kind to each other, tenderhearted, forgiving one another, just as God through Christ has forgiven you. (Ephesians 4:30-32 NLT)*

We are told to get rid of all bitterness, rage, harsh words, and slander. These are examples of evil behavior that bring sorrow to the Holy Spirit. Other translations say, "Do not grieve the Holy Spirit" with these actions. To grieve, in this sense, means to vex, offend, or sadden. By living in bitterness, rage, anger, harsh words, and slander, we offend God and bring sadness to His Spirit. The apostle Paul exhorts us to imitate Christ's kindness and forgiveness.

Are you convinced that bitterness is sin? If not, read a couple more quotes from the Bible:

Their throats are open graves; their tongues practice deceit.
The poison of vipers is on their lips.
Their mouths are full of cursing and bitterness.
Their feet are swift to shed blood;
ruin and misery mark their ways,
and the way of peace they do not know.
There is no fear of God before their eyes.
(Romans 3:13–18 NIV)

This passage describes people who have not believed in Christ. They are not children of God, and they do not have the Holy Spirit. They do not care about pleasing God, as their attitudes and actions prove. The characteristics of their lives include violence, lying, cursing, and bitterness.

Hebrews 12:15 says, "See to it that no one falls short of the grace of God and that no bitter root grows up to cause trouble and defile many" (NIV). Notice that the bitter root defiles "many," not just the troublesome person. This may be a personal sin that starts in the mind and heart, but it is not kept private. People around the bitter person are always affected somehow. It leaks out and causes trouble.

WHERE DID IT COME FROM?

Adults who had difficult childhoods are often tempted to bitterness. Maybe there was divorce and remarriage in the family or perhaps the death of a parent. Maybe financial struggles, substance abuse, or troubled siblings wreaked havoc in the home or monopolized the parents' attention. Maybe the parents were harsh, controlling, or even abusive. Whatever happened, the child was left with deep wounds, a perfect breeding ground for bitterness.

Others may have fallen on hard times after reaching adulthood: a disappointing marriage or other strained relationship, a serious illness, the death of a loved one, the loss of a cherished job, or a career goal thwarted. The common thread here is that when "bad" things happen, they can cause us to be self-pitying, gloomy, and easily hurt. From there it is an easy journey to bitterness.

8

Great Expectations

One of the doorways to bitterness is the pain caused by unmet expectations.

What are expectations? They are things we believe others should do. For example, we expect people to fulfill their obligations. My husband vowed to be faithful to me on our wedding day, and I expect him to keep that promise. If I hired you to do a job, I would expect you to show up on time and perform well. If my light is green and yours is red, I expect you to stop so that I may drive on toward my destination. Failure to comply with any of these expectations will bring consequences.

There are also social expectations. If you are invited to a wedding, you ought to dress appropriately and bring a gift. If you are invited for dinner, you should use good manners, be thankful, and eat the food you are served. At a movie theater, you should sit quietly and silence your phone. These are reasonable and commonly held expectations.

> "To perform a good deed once or twice is easy. But to avoid becoming bitter from the ingratitude and wickedness of those for whom you have done good deeds, that is difficult."
> ~ Martin Luther

However, we can take this further in our imaginations. We can make up our own expectations that are neither reasonable nor obvious to others. If I invite you over for dinner, you may be polite and eat my food, but what if I expect you to bring flowers and compliment my cooking? What if I expect you to return the favor by inviting me to your home? I might be offended by your failure to meet my expectations.

If you give me a gift, it's reasonable to expect a thank you. But what does that look like? If I dash off a quick email, is that good enough? What if you prefer handwritten cards, is that something I should *just know*? Or maybe you excel at making handmade paper and doing calligraphy and are insulted by a mere text message. If my response is not what you imagined it would be, you may become upset with me.

Expectations may be thinly-veiled forms of criticism flowing from pride and selfishness, a way of saying, "I know the best way for you to behave, and you should act accordingly." Like I said earlier, it's appropriate for me to expect my husband to be faithful because he promised he would be, but it's not appropriate to expect him to say or do things that I have imagined and then grow disappointed or angry when he doesn't. We must be extremely cautious with expectations. They can easily become steppingstones to bitterness.

EXAMPLES

What should happen on your wedding anniversary? Should it be just like the jewelry commercials? When you are out for a nice dinner, what should your spouse do and say? How often should you go out? What kind of gifts should you give each other at birthdays and Christmas? If you have expectations but have not communicated them clearly (and realistically) to your spouse, you may be headed for trouble.

How often do young newlyweds find themselves caught in the middle of differing expectations on holidays? One of their mothers may have strong opinions about where and when Thanksgiving dinner is eaten, demanding that everyone celebrates her way. This can easily lead to long-term strife.

Suppose my good friend and I have coffee together every week, and then she gets a new and demanding job. If she can no longer meet as often as before, I may feel hurt or angry. I might think, *I know she is terribly busy, but if the situation were reversed I would certainly make time for our regular appointment. She does not value my friendship as dearly as I value hers.* In my anger, I may push her away and damage an important relationship.

A page from my story:
As you may have guessed by now, Doug did not com-

ply with my expectations, expressed or otherwise. I was hurt. I reasoned that since I have worked in business, I know how a good boss should behave. He should value me in the way I imagined and spend more time with me. He should show appreciation for my talents and gifts in the ways I want him to. Other supervisors used to, why shouldn't he? I didn't allow for the disparity of our temperaments. I wanted him to act like I would act, to do things the way my pride dictated he ought to. Eventually, anger from my unmet expectations became firmly cemented into bitterness.

SETTING EXPECTATIONS VS. SHOWING LOVE

The following chart shows the difference between placing self-centered expectations on others and demonstrating love to others:

Expectations (Selfish)	Love (Unselfish)
In Friendship:	
My friend should call/contact me once a week at minimum.	I haven't heard from my friend in a while. I am going to contact her and see how she is.
My friend should always remember my birthday and make a fuss over it.	I make a point to remember my friend's birthday and make her celebration happy. I show grace if my birthday is ignored.
My friend should always be willing to listen when I need to talk or vent.	I take the time to listen to her even when it's inconvenient for me.
In Church:	
Others should be friendly to me, approach me at church and ask how my week was.	I seek out others, introduce myself and ask questions, show interest in others and seek to bless them.
I should be invited to lunch or dinner every month or so.	I think about who I can invite to lunch or dinner and then do it.
They should remember my prayer needs and ask about my family.	I try to remember details and write down prayer requests. If someone forgets the details of my family or request, I graciously and gently remind them.
They should seek out my talents and gifts and use them in the church, especially gifts of leadership.	I let others know about my gifts, and I wait to be asked or not. I am willing to serve wherever I am needed, even if it's not in the spotlight. I want what is best for the church.

In Marriage:

My spouse should take care of me and make me feel loved.	I seek to bless and show love to my spouse.
Special occasions and vacations should be perfect. My spouse should "go all out" to make it wonderful for me.	I talk honestly about my desires and try to be reasonable with my plans. I am kind if things don't turn out as I had hoped.
My spouse should always follow through on what he/she has promised to do.	I realize that we are all sinners and sometimes we fail. I will offer forgiveness and grace when my spouse disappoints me.

In the Workplace:

My boss should give me the respect and appreciation I deserve.	I will do my work as unto the Lord and show proper respect and submission to the authorities placed over me.
My coworkers should like me and include me in their social plans.	I will model Christ to them and preach the gospel even if it means I am rejected or persecuted.
I should be promoted or given more responsibility as time goes by.	I will be content with the position I am in and seek my identity in Christ.

In Families:

My parents, siblings, and children should treat me with love and respect and give me proper attention (as I define it).	I try to model love to others, offering forgiveness and grace.

My parents should be doting grandparents to my children.	I seek to honor my parents and bless them in obedience to the Lord whether they act as I wish or not.
We should all be together at every holiday.	I want to be with family, but if they have other plans I will accept that without becoming angry.

We need to be compassionate and loving when people don't do things according to our preferences, and we need to spend our time thinking of how to bless others rather than complaining about how they fail to meet our expectations.

9

What Does It Look Like?

CHARACTERISTICS OF BITTERNESS

I believe that people who are especially tempted to bitterness share similar characteristics. Now I'm going to paint a picture for you of how a bitter person acts, speaks, and thinks using my own story and others. Please honestly examine yourself to see if some of these things describe you.

A bitter person overreacts. They become angry very quickly, especially disproportionate to the provocation. They go from zero to sixty in under five seconds. They pile past offenses onto the current offense (or perceived offense) making it seem much larger than it actually is. They punish others way too harshly for the alleged crime. For example, the bitter person might say, "I can't believe she is late...*again!* She is always late! She has no respect for me or my time and always does this to me! I'm sick of it! She's a jerk, and I'm not putting up with her anymore!" Onlookers may think, "So she was a few minutes late. What's the big deal?" but in the mind of the offended, the anger is completely justifiable. If I am bitter against my husband, I may erupt when he fails to hold a door for me. Others may be surprised, after all, it's just the door. But I am thinking, *He always forgets to open the door. We have talked about this over and over which proves he never listens. He has never treated me with the consideration I deserve. He doesn't care about me at all.* I pile all his previous failures onto this one seemingly insignificant event, losing my temper and reacting more severely than the situation warrants. If people are surprised at your level of anger or how quickly you get there, you may be bitter. Sometimes erupting is not possible, say, when in a public setting or if the offender has authority over you. Or you may be the kind of person who just never reacts outwardly, never yelling or causing a scene. Or you may believe, in your self-pitying mind, that to react openly wouldn't make any difference. This is where pouting comes in handy. You might call it "the silent treatment" or freezing someone out. It's still anger, it's just expressed differently. Women are highly adept at this type of behavior, especially with one another. We are taught to act in a "ladylike manner," so we just don't say anything rather than yell or stir up a fuss.

A page from my story

I once had a boss who gave me a very poor annual review. I was shocked and hurt because only weeks earlier he had given me a bonus for exemplary work on a project. I felt utterly betrayed. Of course, since he was my boss I couldn't express this openly, but I did avoid him whenever possible and was extremely cold when I had to interact with him. I also remember passing him in the hallway and pointedly ignoring his greeting to me. I retaliated in anger with the silent treatment because I couldn't vent it openly.

A bitter person uses unkind, accusatory, and extreme terms. The Bible calls this *reviling,* which means to harshly criticize, lambaste, malign, denounce, attack, or pummel. The terms "always" and "never" are generally a part of the tirade.

A bitter person will look for ways to be critical and judgmental. If I'm angry that you failed to keep a promise, I may claim that you're untrustworthy, but I may also accuse you of other things such as laziness or selfishness which have nothing to do with the current situation. I may bring up past instances to prove that you are *always* this way. I may be upset with my husband for a small thing (failing to open the door), but I accuse him of also being a poor listener, forgetful, and uncaring, basically a terrible husband overall.

A page from my story:

Whenever my frustration with Doug boiled over, I would lash out at him in anger. I accused him of callousness and insensitivity. I remember telling him that he had no heart, meaning that he had no concern or compassion for others. This is the man who spends countless hours counseling and encouraging others to love and serve Christ, the man who goes to the hospital in the middle of the night to comfort a family in grief, the man who prayed for me even when I was absolutely nasty to him. Heartless, indeed!

A bitter person accuses others but excuses herself. Bitter people tend to deflect attention away from themselves: "Maybe I was wrong, but let me tell you what *he* did...," or "You don't understand the situation. You don't know what *she* said to me," or "You don't know the whole story here...." This is one of the most evident traits of bitterness, and it comes easily because bitterness is usually a response to the offenses (or perceived offenses) of others. The bitter person might say, "Yes I yelled at my mother-in-law, but she is always criticizing me! I can't ever do anything right in her eyes. She drives me crazy!" She may be sinning, too, but you are excusing your behavior and condemning hers.

A page from my story:

When I was a teenager, I liberally lied to and disobeyed my parents. I knew what the Bible taught, I knew it was wrong, but I felt absolutely no remorse for my actions. Why? I justified it by saying that my parents paid little attention to me and would not allow me to have any friends, fun, or freedom. My only alternative (as I saw it) was to provide them for myself by lying and sneaking around. I justified my failures by pointing to my parents' failures.

A bitter person assumes the worst and looks for evidence to prove his or her assumptions. This is the opposite of what we call "giving the benefit of the doubt" or showing grace. If I ask you not to tease me about an embarrassing incident, and you slip up and make a comment about it, should I immediately pounce and lash out in anger? I can choose to show you grace (maybe you genuinely forgot) or I can explode into assumptions and accusations ("Aha! I knew I couldn't trust you! You probably tell everyone about that. You want to make me look bad.") Or worse yet, I may not have actually asked you not to tease me. I may have just assumed that you knew I wouldn't like it. Perhaps I see a friend talking and laughing with someone, and I decide that she is talking badly about me or making fun of me. I easily assume the worst of her and may become angry. Or if my husband is on a business trip and fails to call me, I may conclude that he doesn't love me because he can't even remember to call. I might even doubt his faithfulness to me. Bitterness takes a minor event and interprets it in the worst possible way.

A page from my story:

Recently, one of our cars was in the repair shop. When it was ready, my husband kindly asked me to take him to pick it up. It made sense that I would drive so that he could just jump out at the shop. However, I refused to drive. Why? Because in the past he has made suggestions about my driving, and I jumped immediately to the conclusion that he would *criticize* me this time, too.

Another page from my story:

Doug occasionally suggested areas of improvement in my work, and I heard, *He doesn't think I'm doing a good job. He doesn't like or respect me. He wishes to be rid of me even though I work so hard.* And then I would sink into self-pity over the great injustice done to me. I took everything to the worst possible conclusion. Even when he complimented me in the same conversation, I only heard the criticism.

A bitter person only accepts their own account of events. They cling to their version of the story even in the face of evidence that proves otherwise. They twist the facts to fit their interpretation, hearing what they choose to hear and ignoring the rest.

Bitter people set up unfair tests:

- "If my husband loved me, he would buy me jewelry on our anniversary. He only brought flowers, therefore he doesn't love me."

- "If the people at church liked me, I would receive a dinner invitation every month."

- "If she really liked me, she would invite me to be on her committee."

Bitter people wallow in self-pity:

- "He says kind things about others but doesn't even notice that I'm here."
- "He never says hello to me."
- "I've been working so faithfully for years and I'm never recognized for my efforts."

Bitter people believe that others conspire against them:

- "He always points out my mistakes but never those of others."
- "He always tries to make me look bad in front of my boss."

Bitter people see what they want to see no matter how irrational it may be.

> *A page from my story:*
> I had decided that Doug did not respect me. I was sure that he did not appreciate my gifts. I couldn't have told you what he should have done to prove that he did, in fact, appreciate me. (Perhaps write a song that said, *We just wouldn't survive without wonderful, talented Linda.* He may have also wept while singing it, but I'm not sure....) But I knew that he despised me, and I would not be convinced otherwise no matter what he said or did. I could not hear a single kind thing he said to me.
> And I couldn't stand to be teased by him. (This is

remarkable because I am always joking and have an overactive sense of humor.) Every time he made a crack, I took it personally and became angry. It was clear proof of his lack of respect for me.

I also decided that his disregard for me had spread to the elder board of our church. I would say to my husband, "The elders all hate me." He would say "Why do you think that?" I had no good answer, I just knew I felt that way. So my dear husband tried logic. He would list a specific elder:

"Does Jay hate you?"

"Well, probably not. He's always very nice," I would say.

"What about Bob?"

"Well, I've known him a long time, he's okay with me."

"How about David?"

"No, he's a dear man. He wouldn't hate anybody."

We would continue on until he had listed almost every member of the board. I couldn't come up with any concrete evidence that any of them had negative feelings toward me. The worst I might prove was indifference. In many cases, they had been very kind and affirming. And yet I was undeterred. I still believed that as a group they disapproved of me. I could see how irrational my thinking was, but it didn't matter. It only increased my irritation with my husband for pointing it out.

A bitter person remembers minute details of an offense and rehearses them often. She can recount every single word of the hurtful things said to her. She knows who said what, what was said in response, what the person did and how and when and why. She replays the video over and over again in her mind until it's memorized. The hurt stays fresh and alive even years later.

A page from my story:

When Doug and I argued, I would often bring up precise words from previous conversations that I could use against him. He would be amazed and frustrated at the specifics I could recall sometimes from years ago. He would say, "How can you remember all this?" My answer should have been, "Because I'm bitter!"

A bitter person is consistently unhappy. I have been in the pit of bitterness, and I can tell you that it is a very dark place. If you know a person who is truly joyful, vibrant, full of gratitude, and loving, you can rightly assume they are not in that pit. Bitter people are genuinely miserable and continually complain while remaining certain that none of their problems are their fault. Unhappiness and even depression can be symptoms and consequences of bitterness.

A bitter person is full of self-pity. This is the seed bed of bitterness. You constantly think about how you have been wronged and poorly treated and how unfair it all is, until sooner or later you are almost completely self-absorbed.

Because of its significance, we will explore this point more thoroughly later.

A page from my story:

I told the story earlier about how my wedding wasn't like other weddings. I didn't get pampered like other brides. Poor me. But here we are almost 30 years later and when I compare my husband with others, I see that I hit the jackpot. No kidding! It's the lifetime after the wedding that really counts, not the fanfare and ceremony of the day. God was abundantly gracious to give me a terrific, godly man who later became an awesome father. Maybe the pictures aren't so hot, but my wedding was great in the way that really matters (which I can clearly see now that I'm no longer blinded by bitterness).

A bitter person desires vengeance (but it never satisfies). Sometimes bitterness grows into outright hatred and violence, sometimes it remains more civilized. Either way, a bitter person wants the other person to get what they deserve. We call it *justice.* Often, we conduct imaginary conversations in our head saying what we wish we could get away with in real life. We may also resort to actual gossip and slander so others will find out the "truth." After all, isn't it only fair that we protect others from this awful person by warning them? But revenge never satisfies. It only leads to more pain and sin. For example, what kind of revenge could I really have gotten against my parents? Could we all go back and relive my childhood? I told them of the pain they caused, but they did not agree. Even if they had, what could they do about it? My bitterness only strained our relationship. I was miserable in my sin, and I inflicted pain on them as well. Or a man might take vengeance on his wife who left him by speaking badly of her to the children. He may blame her for everything and try to garner their sympathy. Even if it were mostly true, his venomous accusations would only result in further division, pain, and estrangement to everyone in the family. He would gain nothing. I have heard the story of a man serving a life sentence for murdering the man who abused his son. Even the ultimate revenge did not satisfy him. He was still bitter. What he needed desperately was repentance and forgiveness for his own sin of bitterness. D. A. Carson writes:

> We cannot live long in this world without coming across injustice, chronic lack of fairness. Many of us accept such sin with reasonable equanimity, reasoning that it is, after all, a fallen world. But when the injustice or unfairness is directed against us, our reaction may be much less philosophical. Then we may nurture a spirit of revenge, or at least of bitterness, malice, and gossip. Such sins in turn assure that our prayers are never more than formulaic; eventually such sin may lead to chronic prayerlessness. "How can I be expected to pray when I have suffered so much?" "Don't talk to me about praying for my enemies: I know who has kept me from being promoted" (*A Call to Spiritual Reformation: Priorities from Paul and His Prayers*, p. 119).

A more common way to take vengeance is to demand an apology. The bitter person says, "I would forgive her if she'd only apologize. But it had better be sincere!" We don't want just *any* apology, we want them to think about what they did, to realize the magnitude of their sin against us, to grovel at our feet, to weep in contrition. Then maybe we will forgive them. We imagine in our minds how sorry they should be, what they should say, how they should say it. If, by chance, we do actually receive an apology, we may be polite and say all the right things, but we won't really forgive because the apology wasn't good enough, or we just know that they didn't really mean it. Even the perfect, most contrite apology (just as we have imagined it) would fail to satisfy because our true desire is revenge not reconciliation.

Bitterness can be transferred, stereotyped, and generalized onto others. If you wound me, I may decide that everyone similar to you will do the same. (And don't try to convince me otherwise! I only believe my own version of events.) I might say, "All the men in my life have let me down, so now I don't trust men," or "A friend at church once betrayed me, so I believe all the people in church are hypocrites," or "My childhood was difficult, therefore I believe the whole world is out to get me."

A page from my story:
   I used to get extremely angry at a restaurant server who was not attentive to me or a salesperson who ignored me. Why? Because I was bitter against my parents. (No kidding!) My thought processes went some-

thing like this: "The waiter ignored me. He found out that I don't matter. He must have gotten the memo that I'm just an unimportant nuisance. See what my parents have done? The whole world hates me." It was crazy! Did my parents ever meet this waiter? How exactly did they influence him? They didn't, of course. That was bitterness and self-pity speaking.

Bitterness rarely stands alone. This is perhaps why it is called a *root* – it gets twisted around and tied up with many other transgressions. Some examples of this entangling might be:

- I spread tales about my friend to warn others about what she is really like (gossip, slander, lying).

- My husband doesn't treat me like Bob treats his wife (jealousy), so I will flirt a little to get some attention (selfishness, immorality). I let him know what a failure he is as a husband and how unhappy I am (anger, reviling). Eventually I may end up being unfaithful, but I couldn't help it – it just happened (adultery).

- My boss doesn't appreciate me or pay me what I'm worth (selfishness, greed) so I'm going to pad my expense accounts, take extra long lunch breaks, and charge things to the company that I feel I deserve (theft).

- My parents divorced and wrecked our family (judgmental pride, selfishness), so I will remove myself and my children from them (unkindness, failure to honor parents).

- God allowed my sister to have cancer and die (lack of faith, trust, and submission to God), so I am going to take out my misery on others (unkindness, selfishness). I will find refuge in some addiction to dull the pain (idolatry).

A bitter person is unconcerned or unaware of how their words and actions affect others. They do not see the pain they cause others. They are oblivious to it. They lash out in anger (Proverbs 12:18) with no care for the damage they cause. They withdraw from friends and loved ones. They make biting, sarcastic remarks. They do this because:

1. They are self-absorbed, not willing to consider the feelings of others. Everything is all about them. If confronted, they would simply say, "He shouldn't be so sensitive. He should know I was only kidding." Or maybe, "I was just venting, she shouldn't take it so seriously. She should just ignore my rants."

2. They believe their words and actions are justified: "I was only defending myself" or "He has hurt me much worse than I hurt him."

The bottom line is that bitter people don't realize how they wound others, or they simply don't care.

A page from my story:

My sister-in-law is very dear to me, I consider her a close friend. However, it did not begin that way. She married my husband's brother and moved to our town, far away from her family and friends, knowing no one but my husband and me. Because of where she is from, I poked fun at her about being a hick from the country. In my mind, I was just teasing her in a good-natured way. I thought I was being funny. She didn't think I was funny. She was lonely, adjusting to a new marriage, and then had to deal with my mockery on top of it. Finally, she had enough and firmly put me in my place with a shocking display of ire.

I had no idea she was so upset by my teasing. If someone had pointed out how unkind I was being, I would have said, "I'm just kidding. She shouldn't be so sensitive!" Then I would have felt hurt and remembered that no one really likes me, and that I always botch everything up, and now my sister-in-law doesn't like me, and she will never like me, et cetera, et cetera. I would have curled up into a selfish ball and descended into oceans of self-pity.

Another page from my story:

Recently while traveling I got stuck in a long line at the security checkpoint. A man was behind me with his wife and two young daughters. He was unhappy about everything. He complained (loudly for all to hear) about how inefficient the TSA was, how this dumb airport was unorganized, how the rental car companies were criminals. He ranted about the government and how this country is full of nitwits. His wife responded with murmurs of agreement and soothing comments. I felt sorry for his family. But then an amazing thing happened.

One of the little girls asked him a question, and in the blink of an eye his demeanor totally changed. He said in a completely different, sweet voice, "Yes, Love?" and then answered her question in that same kind, soft voice. I thought, *Does this man not realize how he is affecting all around him with his loud voice and angry complaints? Why doesn't his wife (and the general public) deserve the same kindness that the little girl does?* He just doesn't realize it. Or if he does, he doesn't care. He is self-consumed and probably bitter, focused on his own frustrations.

10

Bitterness in the Bible

Bitterness is nothing new. The first child ever born on planet earth succumbed to it.

We don't know all the details of why the Lord rejected Cain's offering, but it appears that *Cain* did.

> *The Lord looked with favor on Abel and his offering, but on Cain and his offering he did not look with favor. So Cain was very angry, and his face was downcast. (Genesis 4:4b-5 NIV)*

God's response to Cain's anger was, "If you do what is right, will you not be accepted? But if you do not do what is right, sin is crouching at your door; it desires to have you, but you must master it" (Genesis 4:6-7 NIV).

Cain probably started off with a big pity party, complete with pouting and complaining. He may have railed against God's *unfair* rejection of his offering and turned his jealousy toward his brother. Clearly, he was angry. But God distinctly told him to repent and choose the right thing (which would include putting away his self-pity and bitterness). If he refused, sin would overtake him.

Cain knew the right choice, but he didn't make it. His self-pity, anger, and bitterness eventually led to murder.

KING SAUL

Saul was the first king of Israel. He was tall, handsome, and greatly admired. David was a shepherd boy who became Saul's armor bearer. After his famed killing of the giant Goliath, he became a national hero. Saul heard the women greeting David with a jubilant song:

Saul has slain his thousands, and David his tens of thousands. (1 Samuel 18:7 NIV)

Saul reacted with jealousy and anger. How dare they praise David more than the king himself? 1 Samuel 18:9 reports that "from that time on Saul kept a jealous eye on David." The rest of 1 Samuel documents Saul's further descent into jealousy, bitterness, and repeated attempts to murder David.

By contrast, Saul's son Jonathan became David's most loyal and beloved friend. Remember, Jonathan was Saul's son and heir. If anyone had good reason to be jealous of David and fearful for his future succession in the kingdom, it was Jonathan. As David's popularity grew, it would be understandable if Jonathan felt threatened or attempted to hold onto his own power. But Jonathan chose love, not jealousy or anger against David.

Sadly, Saul's bitterness eventually led to foolishness, which eventually led to his ruin.

MICHAL

The story of Michal and David is one big roller coaster ride. It started out as a love match. When Saul heard that his daughter was in love with David, he saw it as a delightful opportunity to manipulate him. He demanded that David win his betrothed by slaughtering one hundred Philistines, hoping that the young man would fall in battle (1 Samuel 18:25). But David killed *two hundred* men for the love of Michal. What girl wouldn't swoon over that?

After they were married, Michal bravely saved David's life by helping him escape from Saul by tricking him and lying to him. David was on the run for many months. During his absence, Saul forcibly married Michal to another man. Scripture doesn't record her reaction, but she was probably quite unhappy. One wonders what she thought: Was she expecting David to come back and rescue her? Did she think he should arrange for her escape? Perhaps as time passed, she was greatly disappointed in David and believed he no longer loved her.

During the next years, David traveled with his men, avoiding Saul and gathering more followers and wives along the way. After Saul died and David became king over Judah, he lived in Hebron for seven years where he had six sons by six different wives (2 Samuel 3:2-5). One could easily surmise that he had forgotten all about Michal.

And then suddenly he demanded her return. He didn't fetch her himself, but sent Abner to get her, like a piece of property (2 Samuel 3:13-14). The next scene is just comical. Michal was stolen away from her husband Paltiel who followed, weeping, all the way to the next town. Abner rebuked him and forced him to return home like a kicked puppy.

It appears that Paltiel loved her, but did she love him? Was she sad to be leaving him? Was she anxious to return to David? We don't know what was going on in her heart at this time, but later we see a drastic change in her.

After David became king over all Israel and defeated the Philistines, he triumphantly brought the Ark of the Covenant back to Jerusalem. It was a grand festival, a public celebration with music and dancing and sacrifices, with David dancing before the Lord in worship. As Michal watched from her window, it says she "despised him in her heart" (2 Samuel 6:16). The girl who desperately loved David and risked her life for him now despises him. Why? Was she embarrassed by him? Jealous of him?

Afterward, when he came in to bless his household (which implies an audience), she spewed her venom on him publicly. She sarcastically rebuked him for acting like a vulgar fellow during the celebrations. She tried to shame him. It seems like a case of way too much anger to fit the offense. Bitterness had grown in her heart and probably had been there for some time.

Why was she bitter? Perhaps she had grown to love Paltiel and was happy with him. Perhaps she felt objectified by being snatched away and returned to David. Perhaps she still loved David but was hurt that he had forgotten her. Perhaps she was jealous of the other wives and their children. Whatever her motivation, her harsh words demonstrated deep resentment toward him.

And there were consequences:

> *And Michal daughter of Saul had no children to the day of her death. (2 Samuel 6:23 NIV)*

We don't know whether this was because God closed her womb or due to David's abandonment of her. We do know this was the greatest sorrow and shame a married woman in that culture could face.

Poor Michal really was wronged in this story. She was used as a pawn between Saul and David, and both she and Paltiel were hurt in the process. David surely doesn't win any awards for being a considerate and devoted husband, but how she reacted was her sin and her responsibility before God. Her bitterness caused her to speak rashly against God's anointed king who was also her husband. It led to her barrenness.

NAOMI

In the book of Ruth, we read of Naomi who lost her husband and both sons in the foreign land of Moab. After many years away, she traveled back home to Israel with her daughter-in-law Ruth. When they got there, Naomi complained to everyone that God had wronged and afflicted her. She even told them to call her "Bitter." She never mentioned her loyal and kind daughter-in-law who left home and family to travel with her. She only focused on the negative, what she had lost and Who was to blame:

> *So the two women went on until they came to Bethlehem. When they arrived in Bethlehem, the whole town was stirred because of them, and the women exclaimed, "Can this be Naomi?" "Don't call me Naomi," (which means pleasant) she told them. "Call me Mara, (which means bitter) because the Almighty has made my life very bitter. I went away full, but the LORD has brought me back empty. Why call me Naomi? The LORD has afflicted (or testified against) me; the Almighty has brought misfortune upon me." (Ruth 1:19-21 NIV)*

Later in the story, Naomi took Ruth's son and cared for him. The local women rejoiced with her and said, "Naomi has a son!" (Ruth 4:17). It never records that Naomi gave thanks for the great blessings she received or repented of her bitterness.

It seems that with increased age comes a greater temptation to bitterness. Or perhaps long-ingrained habits are harder to break as time goes on. This may have been Naomi's struggle. Surely, some kind words to Ruth would have been appropriate. And giving praise and thanksgiving to God would have been the proper response at the end of this story. But perhaps her spite was so firmly ingrained that eventually she could no longer see it, leaving her unable to repent or be grateful.

EUODIA AND SYNTYCHE

In his letter to the church at Philippi, the apostle Paul asked a friend to help two women—Euodia and Syntyche—work toward reconciliation:

> *I entreat Euodia and I entreat Syntyche to agree in the Lord. Yes, I ask you also, true companion, help these women, who have labored side by side with me in the gospel together with Clement and the rest of my fellow workers, whose names are in the book of life. (Philippians 4:2-3 ESV)*

We don't have much information about their situation, but here are some things we can surmise: Paul loved both Euodia and Syntyche and considered them his fellow workers in the spread of the gospel. They had been coworkers on Clement's team. Their names are in the book of life (i.e. both women were believers). Their disagreement was well-known and becoming a distraction within the church. They couldn't resolve this by themselves. They needed someone to mediate.

Reading between the lines, it appears that bitterness had taken root – neither woman would budge. Others were probably affected if not taking sides. The potential for personal strife and congregational factions was high. This conflict was a big enough concern in the Philippian church that Paul felt it needed to be addressed.

A practical lesson for us is that sometimes we need help to

deal with our anger and bitterness. We should not be afraid to get a trusted friend involved, someone who can see our situation more clearly. Bitterness is sin, but it is not unforgivable or unresolvable. Repentance and reconciliation are possible. That is always the desired outcome.

A page from my story:

When Doug and I were struggling to get along, I sought help from another elder and his wife. They lovingly listened to me complain about him, and then gently suggested that I was bitter. I had heard the same accusation from Doug himself many times, but I could not accept it because of how bitterness blinded me. It was necessary for me to hear the truth from an objective third party. Just as importantly, I felt cared for and accepted by them, not judged. Eventually, Doug and I met with them together and it helped greatly. We needed others to come alongside us.

11

Bitter Consequences

And now we come to the painful part that may motivate our change—consequences. All sin has consequences of some sort, either just within us or, more often, affecting others as well. God has promised to forgive our sin if we repent and ask (1 John 1:9), but there are lingering consequences that follow us.

UNHAPPINESS/DEPRESSION/JOYLESSNESS

Bitterness is sin. Sin depresses our spirit. It weighs us down and drives a wedge between us and God. It robs us of happiness and freedom. Bitter people are not happy, and they blame everyone else for that.

The effects of sin are described in the Psalms:

> *O Lord, rebuke me not in your anger,*
> *Nor discipline me in your wrath!*

For your arrows have sunk into me,
And your hand has come down on me.

There is no soundness in my flesh
Because of your indignation;
There is no health in my bones
Because of my sin.

For my iniquities have gone over my head;
Like a heavy burden, they are too heavy for me.

My wounds stink and fester
Because of my foolishness,

I am utterly bowed down and prostrate;
All the day I go about mourning.

For my sides are filled with burning,
And there is no soundness in my flesh.

I am feeble and crushed;
I groan because of the tumult of my heart.
Psalm 38:1-8 ESV

Heavy burden...festering wounds...a tumult of the heart...that's what it feels like to be embroiled in bitterness. It's a genuine experience of feeling hurt. I can tell you that sometimes I wanted to burst. I wanted to scream to the world, "Don't you see what's going on? Can't you see the injustice done to me? Why can't I ever be treated nicely like others are? It's so unfair! You don't know what they are really like!"

But you are the one who is most miserable, not the person who has wronged you. Maybe you've heard the phrase, "eaten up with bitterness." It's an accurate assessment. It consumes one's joy for life. Bitter people are not lighthearted or glad. They are not loving or content. (And, usually, they are not popular with others.) Both Doug and my husband Dave said to me many times, "You are never happy." It was true. Even when they tried to gratify me with kind words or actions, it was never enough. I could not be satisfied.

In the past, when someone referred to bitterness, I envisioned a cranky old woman, someone who hates life, hates everyone around her, has nothing but complaints and criticism on her tongue; she is covered with wrinkles from frowning, and her mouth is twisted like a sour raisin. That is not far from the truth. It is what you and I could become but for the grace of God. It is what I was well on my way to becoming.

HARSH AND UNKIND SPEECH

As Jesus taught in Luke 6:45, your words reveal what is in your heart. If your heart is full of grace, your words will show it. If your heart is full of resentment, your words will overflow accordingly.

The good man brings good things out of the good stored up in his heart, and the evil man brings evil things out of the evil stored up in his heart. For out of the overflow of his heart his mouth speaks. (Luke 6:45 NIV)

The tongue has the power of life and death, and those who love it will eat its fruit. (Proverbs 18:21 NIV)

One of the easiest ways to determine if a person is bitter is to talk to them. What they say and how they say it will usually betray their malicious attitude toward someone. They will have a difficult time saying kind words about the object of their spite. I know this from experience. Many of the sins I committed while engulfed in bitterness included unkind things I said to or about others. (By the way, typing is also a way of "speaking." Your keystrokes reveal what is in your heart in the same way that the tongue does.)

A page from my story:

With Doug, things came out of my mouth that I wasn't expecting or intending to say. I would make nasty little comments, veiled insults, and hints of criticism, usually in a sarcastic or "joking" manner. I couldn't seem to help myself. Sometimes, I would think, "Where did that come from?" It was clear evidence of the bitterness lurking in my heart. Those who knew me best could see it.

SELF-RIGHTEOUSNESS

When we focus on how wrong others are, we start to think that we look good by comparison. ("I would never behave like *that*.") We develop judgmental and critical tendencies. We think we know the best way to do things, that we have the best idea. We set up expectations we think others should fulfill. We say things like, "I am raising my kids much better than my parents raised me. I would never make the mistakes they did." Or, "If I were in charge of this department, I would be a better supervisor than my boss." Or, "Why don't they listen to my opinions? They don't value my intelligence and experience, that's why!" Or, "I am a great wife, but my husband still doesn't treat me as I deserve." Or, "I do so many kind and helpful things around this church but nobody notices or appreciates me."

This is all pride, plain and simple. God opposes proud people (James 4:6).

ESTRANGEMENT FROM PEOPLE

A bitter person goes to great lengths to avoid and ignore the person they are bitter against. If I am bitter, I will do everything in my power to stay away from you. I may also pout or give you the cold shoulder. This gets complicated because, in most cases, the one I'm bitter against is someone regularly involved in my life: a spouse, relative, friend, boss, coworker. But I will find a way. I will say, "I am sick and tired of putting up with him." Or, "I am done with this relationship." Or, "I'm never calling her again!"

A loving person would attempt to reconcile. Love draws close – bitterness pushes apart: couples stop talking and start sleeping in separate bedrooms, friends stop spending time together and grow apart.

If you persist in bitterness, you will have less people to share it with as time goes on. People will separate themselves from you. You will be increasingly unattractive, and I'm not referring to physical characteristics. Nobody will want to listen to your version of *It's not fair!* or *The world is against me!* for the thousandth time. Even if some are sympathetic and listen to you for hours upon hours, it will not be enough. Eventually they will tire of your vitriol. This sounds harsh, but it's true. Unless you have a common enemy (someone you are both bitter against), people will distance themselves from you.

ESTRANGEMENT FROM GOD

Unconfessed sin separates us from God:

> *If I had cherished sin in my heart, the Lord would not have listened. (Psalm 66:18 NIV)*

> *But your iniquities have made a separation between you and your God, and your sins have hidden his face from you so that he does not hear. (Isaiah 59:2 ESV)*

God promises to forgive us when we confess our sin to Him, but when we refuse to confront it, or we downplay it, He will not fellowship with us.

Many times, we get comfortable in our sin. It's "just the way we are," we reason. This puts up a major roadblock in our spiritual growth and hinders our prayer life. As D.A. Carson says, "Many of us do not want to pray because we know that disciplined, biblical prayer would force us to eliminate sin that we rather cherish. It is very hard to pray with compassion and zeal for someone we much prefer to resent" (*A Call to Spiritual Reformation*, p. 119).

SELFISHNESS AND SELF-PITY

With bitterness, the story is all about *me—how they hurt me, what they did to me, how I was wronged, ignored, insulted, how my rights were disregarded, my feelings were hurt, my desires weren't fulfilled.* And it's everyone else's fault. Those who are excessively self-focused can easily fall into bitterness.

It goes the other way, too. Holding on to bitterness leads to increased self-pity. "Nothing ever works out for me," comes the complaint. Then we retreat into a cocoon of self-protection.

Habits are hard to break. If you continually focus on yourself and all the injustices done to you, your mind learns that pattern.

> **Will not a tiny speck very close to our vision blot out the glory of the world, and leave only a margin by which we see the blot? I know no speck so troublesome as self.**
> **~ George Eliot**

You automatically revert to that way of thinking when something unpleasant occurs. Your world becomes smaller as your focus narrows. It becomes increasingly difficult to think about others, much less love them or do good to them.

But selfishness and self-pity are sin.

This is fairly new information for me. I never thought it was wrong to indulge in a little pity party from time to time. It's not like my *Poor Me!* wallowing was hurting anyone. Besides, if I didn't feel sorry for myself, who would?

Why is it sin? Because it puts me on the throne instead of Christ. It focuses love and attention inward—*my* desire, *my* hurt, *my* pain, what *I* wish would happen, *my* plan to get what *I* want—rather than outward toward others and, most importantly, toward Jesus. I worship at the altar of "me" which constitutes idolatry because it robs Jesus of the adoration and gratitude He should receive. This is serious business! If you think God doesn't mind a little idolatry, just read through the Old Testament. Israel was warned repeatedly and punished harshly for worshipping other gods. We must be aware of how offensive this sin is.

Remember my picture of the bitter old lady? She spends her days alone feeling sorry for herself and blaming everyone else. She is the only attendee at her own elaborate (*sinful*) pity party.

CONTAGION

Remember the aspen roots! If a man is bitter toward someone, he often infects his wife, tempting her to bitterness, too. In churches, ill will can spread quickly across a congregation causing gossip and dissension. In companies, employees can spend every lunch hour and coffee break criticizing the management and spreading acrimony around the office. And I may take up a friend's cause and become angry at her husband on her behalf.

Bitterness can be the family legacy. A mother's attitude toward her husband will be picked up by her children. Children can be hostile toward their parents, and parents toward their children. If conflict is not handled well, it can foster strife in the whole household.

A page from my story:

In my family, we would get angry and argue and shout, then retreat to our respective corners in silence. Eventually, communication resumed, but the blowup was never discussed or resolved. No one admitted blame or sought reconciliation. The incident was simply forgotten. Of course, it was not really forgotten, so when a new conflict occurred, it piled onto the previous one, adding one more reason to be mad and to blame each other. This pattern led straight to bitterness because we never gave or received forgiveness. We learned to revisit and rehearse the past, to reassign blame, and to become angry again and again.

I have heard stories about my great-grandmother's conflict with her sister over the latter's marriage. They had lived together and run a business. After the wedding, they did not speak again for the rest of their lives. What a sad and tragic tale of bitterness! Who knows how far back this heritage goes? I am determined to leave a different legacy to my children by making sure that we discuss problems and work toward godly resolution through repentance and for-giveness. I want to model this, which means admitting when I am wrong and asking for their forgiveness when necessary. If we don't break the pattern, it will continue to be passed on, leaving a wake of pain and sin behind.

UNWANTED GUEST

Therefore each of you must put off falsehood and speak truthfully to your neighbor, for we are all members of one body. "In your anger do not sin": Do not let the sun go down while you are still angry, and do not give the devil a foothold. (Ephesians 4:25-27 NIV)

Matthew Henry comments on this: "We give place to the devil, when the first motions of sin are not grievous to our souls; when we consent to them."

When we downplay bitterness as "not *that* bad," we open the door wide for the devil to come in. We give him access to other areas and free rein in our hearts. Remember, he is a roaring lion waiting to devour us, not a gentle kitten nipping at our heels (1 Peter 5:8). He wants to consume us, to kill us! He

"The Devil is easy to invite as a guest, but hard to get rid of." ~ Martin Luther

wants our faith to be completely dead and useless for the Kingdom of God. Although he cannot separate us from God's love (Romans 8:31-39), he can weigh us down, cause us to feel defeated, and severely reduce our fruitfulness. Consider rock climbing. The climber moves from handhold to foothold, making his way up the wall. To take away his foothold would greatly impede his progress. He would be stuck at that spot until he could find another way or make a new foothold. If we provide the enemy ample footholds, he will merrily scamper up our walls and do all kinds of damage. Anger makes his climb easy and fast.

A page from my story:

My husband tells me (to my shame) that I was unkind to my children. I'm sure I was often spiteful toward him, too, and I know I was awful to Doug. With Doug, I reasoned that he didn't care what I thought, that he didn't have feelings, so that my words and actions didn't bother him. Not true! I wounded him in ways I didn't realize. With my husband, I justified my unkindness by hanging on to the pain he caused me through his failures in some areas. (Pain does not excuse sin— sinning makes the pain worse.)

During one of my lowest points, I became irate before a church service and lashed out at several members of my beloved worship team. I wasn't angry with them specifically, just upset and generally miserable, and they received the brunt of it. I was deeply sorry and apologized afterwards, but the overflow of my black heart had leaked out and caused damage that I did not intend.

LIFELONG

I said earlier that bitterness remembers details. Those memories will last a lifetime if we allow them to. If you hear an older person talk about their past, you can often tell if they are harboring bitterness. Their stories will be colored with how people wronged them or how unfair things were. They will not be grateful for much.

This happens as regrets about what can't be changed become resentment over lost opportunities. We blame others for what we feel we missed out on. We lament things we didn't try or risks we didn't take. An older woman despises her husband for not giving her the marriage she always dreamed of and her children for not living how she wanted them to (such as marrying the right person or giving her grandchildren). An older man is grumpy and difficult because of physical limitations and illness. They both blame God for taking their friends or loved ones in death, leaving them lonely and desolate. Who wants to be the last one left?

Rage begun in youth will become *more* furious, not less, as time goes by. Bitterness will build into destructive habits and a lifestyle of anger and discontentment if it is not overcome. How can we possibly change the way we react or the way we feel? Read on, dear friend. There is hope.

PART III

What Can I Do About It?

12

Where to Start

How do you feel about God? How does He feel about you? What is your relationship with Him like? What do you believe about Him? Your answers to these basic questions are crucial for overcoming bitterness. If you are not a Christian, the following section will show you how to find grace and hope in Jesus Christ. Please read it carefully and honestly, and if you have questions, seek out a Christian friend or pastor to help you work through it. If you are a Christian, be reminded again of who Jesus is and why you need Him so desperately.

YOU NEED SOME GOOD NEWS

God reveals Himself to us through the Holy Bible. In it we learn that God created the entire universe. He is the preeminent Being, the most wise, powerful, and sovereign King. He knows absolutely everything that can be known. Our abilities to breathe, walk, talk, or even think are only possible because

He sustains our life moment by moment, day by day (Acts 17:28). We owe everything about our existence to Him. His greatness is beyond our comprehension. And yet, He pursues a relationship with us (John 3:16).

But there is a problem. How can a perfectly righteous and good God be friends with people who have rebelled against Him? That's what we are, you see, *rebels*. All of us. We have all disobeyed His rules. No one has ever been perfectly good (Romans 3:23). No one has ever done everything that God wanted him or her to do. This is bad news because the Bible also says that "the wages of sin is death" (Romans 6:23). This means that we all deserve God's wrath, that we should all be punished because of our disobedience. The "salary" God will pay for the evil things we have done is eternal punishment and separation from Him in Hell, a place of torment, pain, and unparalleled loneliness (Revelation 20:15). Bad news indeed!

But there is hope.

The second part of Romans 6:23 says that if we believe in His Son Jesus Christ, God will give us a free gift—forgiveness of all our sins and life with Him in Heaven forever after we die. Everyone who believes "the gospel" receives that gift, the gift of salvation.

Gospel is simply a word that means "good news." The good news goes like this: Jesus is God's Son. He was born to a virgin named Mary over 2,000 years ago. He lived a perfect life in complete obedience to God. But He died on a cross—punished by God even though He had done nothing wrong. Why? Because God treated Jesus as though He were an evil sinner, as though He were you or me. This is what it means when the Bible says that Jesus died "for our sins" (1 Corinthians 15:3). He was punished as a substitute for us, and His perfect obedience is put to our account, so to speak, so that now God treats us as though we actually do everything right, as though we were Jesus (2 Corinthians 5:21). Do you see what this does to our sins? They are gone, eradicated, completely forgiven (Psalm 103:12).

But here is the key. There is only one way to get this forgiveness. We have to admit to God that we have disobeyed Him. We have to admit that we deserve His punishment. And we have to ask Him for forgiveness.

And we have to believe the whole story of Jesus which does not end with His death on the cross. Two days later, He came back to life (1 Corinthians 15:4). Then He went back up to Heaven to live with God until God sends Him back to earth to judge everyone.

That is what you must believe. If you do, and if you ask God for forgiveness, all of your sins will be forgiven forever. If that happens, something else also happens – your desires will change. You will want to live the rest of your earthly life loving, worshipping, and obeying Jesus. You will want to live in a way that pleases Him. (There is more to tell, but that is the essential part.)

You may wonder why God would do this. That answer is simple. It is because He is loving and merciful. He knew that we had no hope without Him, so He chose to show us grace.

But God demonstrates his own love for us in this: While we were still sinners, Christ died for us. (Romans 5:8 NIV)

THE DIFFERENCE JESUS MAKES

Once we have trusted Christ to pay the penalty for our sins, the Bible says that we are new creatures (2 Corinthians 5:17). The old, wicked person we were is no more. Or to put it another way, we are adopted into God's family (Romans 8:12-17). As His children, we begin to act more like Him: good, righteous, and loving. This is true because God fills us with His Spirit who changes us from the inside out (Galatians 5:16-17). As strange as it may sound, His Spirit dwells within us all the time, with all of His comfort, guidance, and power. God is literally with us at all times.

This is also good news because it means that we can change. We don't have to continue in sin. We are not trapped in our bitterness. God will help us to become different. With God's Spirit living inside us, we have the power to defeat sin. We have the power to live as new creatures.

Those who have the Spirit look and act differently from those who don't. Their lives produce a different kind of fruit. In Galatians 5:22-23, the evidences of God's Spirit are listed: love, joy, peace, patience, kindness, goodness, faithfulness, gentleness, and self-control. Bitter people don't have these things. They are not filled with joy. They don't live peacefully or gently. They are not kind toward others. They are only faithful to themselves. And they are out of control emotionally, mentally, and verbally. But with the help of God's

Spirit, all of that can change. We can be transformed into radically different creatures.

1 John 4:7 says, "Beloved, let us love one another, for love is from God, and whoever loves has been born of God and knows God" (ESV). Love is listed as defining evidence of being a child of God. Those who abide in Christ love others. Bitterness is the opposite of love. In 1 Corinthians 6:10, it is listed alongside other serious sins: adultery, idolatry, drunkenness, homosexuality. Now if you look at that verse in your Bible, you won't find the word *bitterness*, you will find *revile* instead, which means to criticize in an abusive or angry and insulting manner. You might call it "telling somebody off." It's bitterness that comes out in our words. And notice, it's in the same category as adultery. It's bad. It's unloving. And it must change for the beloved children of the King. We must be kind and gracious just like our Father who forgave our sins.

In summary, the fight against bitterness starts with knowing and believing the gospel which brings forgiveness and the power to change who we are and what we want. God's love for us, proven at the cross of Jesus, will move us to love Him. Love for Him will show in our love for others. Bitterness is only love for self which has to go if we are going to be like our loving Father.

13

The Remedy for Bitterness

The remedy for bitterness is love, the kind mentioned in 1 Peter 4:8: "Above all, keep loving one another earnestly, since love covers a multitude of sins" (ESV). Notice it says to keep loving *earnestly*. We are to keep at it, to persist in it, to work hard at it, to devotedly and actively love others. This is not a fluffy *feeling* we can just conjure up at will. (If it were that easy, nobody would be stuck in bitterness.) No, love is a verb, an activity, a choice we make. If someone has hurt you, you must work tirelessly to forgive and love them.

And you can't pretend to do it. You must truly love. Romans 12:9-10 says, "Love must be sincere. Hate what is evil; cling to what is good. Be devoted to one another in love. Honor one another above yourselves" (NIV). Notice the extremes: hating one thing, clinging to another, honoring someone else above yourself. This all sounds rather like much is at stake (and it is!). This is not a nonchalant command to try and get along by producing a peaceful, loving feeling in our hearts. This is an imperative to *hate – shun – abhor – loathe* the evil that is the opposite of love, and *cling to – stick to – hang on tightly to – embrace* the good that pleases God.

Jesus commanded us to love God with all our heart, soul, mind, and strength, and to love our neighbors as much as we love ourselves (Matthew 22:37-39). The second part assumes that we already love ourselves (and oh, what a great love it is!). But Christ must be our first love, our first priority, our first thought. How often do we really do this? Instead, how often do we think of ourselves first?

It works like this—if my entire life were outward-focused, if I loved God and others, I would never be selfishly hurt or angry and never sink into bitterness. I would accept God's plan for my life (including necessary trials and sorrows). I would want everyone else to be blessed (even those people I don't naturally like). I would desire for God's Kingdom to advance (despite great personal cost, discomfort, and inconvenience). I would love my brothers and sisters by serving them, building them up, and speaking kindly to them. When we genuinely love God, we never regret living for His glory alone. It's not settling for second best or being a doormat or missing out on the pleasures of life. He has promised to give us good things and an abundant life full of joy (Matthew 6:33). We won't miss out on anything truly worth having. What a comforting promise!

Love *covers* the sins of others. When someone speaks thoughtlessly to you, you can choose to bury it under love for them. Go out in the yard, dig up shovelfuls of dirt, and cover that offense. If it's buried deeply enough, you won't see it or smell it again. As time goes by, it will even be hard to find the spot where it was buried. Weather and vegetation will have smoothed it over. You might even plant flowers over it. This is your persistent, intentional effort to be devoted to them and honor them above yourself.

Sometimes this is described as just "letting it go," a phrase that used to drive me crazy. But now I've changed my mind. I was talking to someone recently about this concept of letting it go. I told her I didn't like it, that I couldn't relate to it. But then God gave me a new picture. Imagine holding tightly to something, clutching it firmly against your chest. Imagine holding it with two clenched fists. If you are asked to let it go, you open your hands and drop it, placing your open palms outward. This posture is an attitude of surrender. You're saying, "I give up! I don't want to fight anymore!" Who are you surrendering to? Your gracious Savior, of course. You are saying "I will do it Your way, Lord!" And then let's take that posture a bit further. Your hands are out in front of you in surrender, now lift them higher. You're in a posture of worship. Now it's all about Jesus. It's a way of saying, "I surrender to you, Lord. I give up this hurt and pain, and I worship You for all You've done in my life." (Spend a minute worshipping right now. He is worthy! Psalm 96:4)

LOVE VS. BITTERNESS

Love is patient, love is kind. It does not envy, it does not boast, it is not proud. It does not dishonor others, it is not self-seeking, it is not easily angered, it keeps no record of wrongs. Love does not delight in evil but rejoices with the truth. It always protects, always trusts, always hopes, always perseveres. Love never fails. (1 Corinthians 13:4–8 NIV)

Now compare that side by side with bitterness:

Love	Bitterness
Is patient	Flies off the handle easily: "I can't believe he did that again! They always/never..."
Is kind	Is mean, accusing, unfair
Does not envy	Is jealous: "Why didn't I get that job/husband/talent like she did? Why do people pay more attention to her?"
Does not boast	Insists: "I am better than she is. I don't do _____ like she does."
Is not proud	Is self-righteous: "I treat people better than he does."
Does not dishonor others	Tries to turn public opinion against others, either subtly or overtly (through gossip)
Is not self-seeking or selfish	Totally focuses on *me*, *my* rights, *my* hurts, the wrong done to *me*, wallowing in self-pity
Is not easily angered	Is easily angered, a spark just waiting to explode
Keeps no record of wrongs	Remembers every single detail of every wrong ever committed or perceived
Does not delight in evil	Wants payback, revenge, or justice
Rejoices with the truth	Hangs on to *my* version of the truth, and will not accept any alternate version, no matter how clearly or objectively it is presented
Protects	Seeks to harm and humiliate
Trusts	Does not trust, always waiting and watching for that person to slip up and offend me, expects the worst

Hopes, perseveres, never fails	Distances oneself, estranges, and says, "I am done with her."

This must be taken seriously. John calls us liars if we claim to love God and yet hate our brothers or sisters (1 John 4:20). Although we don't want to admit it, bitterness toward someone is nothing short of hatred. We are not bitter because we love them, are we? Jesus commands us to love others like He loved us (John 15:12-13), sacrificially and selflessly. When we downplay or rationalize away our bitterness (or lack of love), we are disobeying God and avoiding the truth. If we are not willing to come to terms with our sin, we may not even be true followers of Jesus.

14

The Path to Freedom

So how exactly do you overcome this sin of bitterness? We have said it is only through the power of God's Spirit working in us, but we have steps to take, too. What are they? The following will help guide anyone who seriously desires to change.

#1 Repent. Tell God that you realize your bitterness is sin. Ask Him to forgive you and to help in the ongoing battle.

In my experience, bitterness requires constant vigilance, repeated repentance, and lots of painful digging. (Think of the aspen roots!) The Bible says, "Get rid of all bitterness, rage and anger, brawling and slander, along with every form of malice" (Ephesians 4:31 NIV). Confess to God that you have been involved in evil behavior by harboring bitterness. And if you have been bitter at God for what He has allowed in your life, you must confess that to Him as well, and repent of it.

#2 Choose to forgive those you are bitter against. You

can't do this on your own. Ask God to help you. (We will discuss forgiveness in more depth later.)

#3 Repeat 1 & 2. Tomorrow you will have to do both of these things again. (And the next day, and the next....)

#4 Ask for help from godly leaders. James 5:14 says, "Is anyone among you sick? Let him call for the elders of the church, and let them pray over him, anointing him with oil in the name of the Lord" (NIV). The word *sick* (Gr. *astheneo*) means "to be weak." It includes not only physical weakness, but spiritual weakness as well. Being caught up in bitterness surely qualifies as a weakness. It is a major spiritual battle going on in our minds and hearts. We need to ask our spiritual leaders to pray for us.

I did this after I began to understand the magnitude of my sin. It wasn't easy. I felt ashamed, embarrassed, and somewhat fearful. After all, I'm in leadership. I should know better, right? And what if my elders hear how awful I've been and decide to get rid of me? But I knew I was really stuck. I saw that I was in sin, but I didn't understand what it was or see how I could ever get over it. I went to them and said something like, "I'm so bitter and angry; help!" I then sobbed while they prayed.

James 5:15-16 says, "And the prayer of faith will save the one who is sick (weak), and the Lord will raise him up. And if he has committed sins, he will be forgiven. Therefore, confess your sins to one another and pray for one another, that you may be healed" (ESV). I am a testimony to God's faithfulness to His Word. I have been healed!

#5 Ask for accountability. Talk regularly with someone

who will encourage you in this battle with sin. Like aspen roots, bitterness can become firmly grown into our hearts and become a habitual reaction. This is not usually an easy or overnight fix. When bitterness would spew from my mouth, my husband fulfilled this role for me by gently asking questions like, "Is that true? Is that fair? Is that bitterness?" It helped (even if I did not always appreciate it at the moment).

#6 Pray, pray, pray. Ask the Lord to increase your love for Him and for others. Ask Him to give you a gracious and forgiving spirit. Take steps to bless those you were formerly bitter against, and pray for them. Pray for anyone you struggle to forgive. Pray for their family and their job. Pray for their sanctification if they are a believer and their salvation if they are not. Pray for yourself. Remember, the remedy to bitterness is love. Love is an action, not just a feeling. Sometimes the feelings follow more readily if you begin with an action. I may not feel like showing you love, but if I start down the path with a tangible act of blessing, my feelings will eventually catch up. Start small—say something kind to or about the person you've been harboring bitterness against. You can eat an entire elephant if you take enough small bites.

#7 Deal quickly with anger. Resolve conflicts immediately. Don't let offenses pile up into bitterness.

Ephesians 4:26b says, "Don't let the sun go down while you are still angry" (NLT). But what if the conflict begins at night? What does this really mean? The Greek words here imply a very short time which most scholars agree is no longer than approximately two days. I am to deal with this conflict and resolve it by either repenting or forgiving within that time. If I stay angry longer than two days, I'm sliding into bitterness. If I recall events that happened last week, I'm sinning.

#8 Fight the daily war in the battlefield of your mind. Martin Luther once said, "Thoughts damage not the brain but the heart." A large part of this battle against bitterness takes place in our soft grey matter. This is why we can sometimes conceal bitterness. It's just going on inside our minds. (Until we open our mouths, that is.) God promises the power to live a righteous life which includes control over our thoughts, words, and actions.

How do we fight this battle? Here are some suggestions:

Put on the armor of God (Ephesians 6:11). The enemy will attack you in this area, be sure of that. We can't overcome sin, live a godly life, or forgive others without the Holy Spirit of God working in our hearts, so we must be prepared to fight. We must be in the Word of God regularly, stay accountable to our Christian brothers and sisters, pray and ask God to strengthen us through His Spirit.

Put up "No Trespassing" signs. Rope off areas in your mind that you will not visit again. (Not allowed to go there! No rehearsing!) Perhaps you often think back on your childhood with bitterness, recalling how things should have been different or remembering things you were deprived of. You look at other families wistfully and think that's what you deserved. Maybe your marriage is a constant temptation. In the culture we live in, romance is idolized. Every girl dreams of a fairy-tale wedding and happily ever after. This will not happen here on earth until that day that we are united with our ultimate Bridegroom, Jesus Christ. Only He can provide the perfect wedding and happily ever after ending with Him in Heaven. But you can decide that you're not going to think about what you wish your wedding was like, or what your marriage could have been, if only…. *No going there. Ever!*

For instance, you say, "I have forgiven my mother for criticizing me. I will not hold that against her any more." The next time she calls, you will not be waiting for the criticism to drip from her lips. If she sins again, you will forgive her again. You will not let it accrue. You won't go back and think about the many times she's done that or how unfair it is, and you will not rehearse every hurtful thing she's said. It's forgiven and done.

> *A page from my story:*
>
> Every time people talk about their childhood memories, I am tempted to remember my own with bitterness. Whenever weddings are discussed, or photo albums are brought out, I fight the temptation to resent my wedding. I have asked the Lord to make that a fallow field in my mind. It's not to become fertile. With the help of the Holy Spirit, it will never be planted again. It's roped off, deserted, and won't be revisited. I can, however, visit the list of my parents' many admirable qualities: they helped us buy our first car, they gave us a loan for our first house, they forgave part of that loan after we were in the process of paying it back. Few people have parents so generous and gracious.

Compile a list of truth. Bitterness believes only its own version of events. Remind yourself of the good or kind things about the person or events you're tempted to be bitter about. For example, my parents are very generous. They have helped me out financially. And one of the blessings they gave to me as a child was modeling a faithful devotion to the church and God's people. I should reflect on those successes rather than on what I perceive to be their failures. Ask God to give you truth to reflect on when you are tempted. Write it down and refer to it often.

A page from my story:

Years ago I had a particularly awful meeting with Doug and several others. I thought the purpose of the meeting was to calmly discuss and resolve our ongoing differences, but it went terribly wrong. I felt unfairly accused and deeply humiliated. My anger and bitterness grew exponentially after that meeting. I was sure I would never be able to get over it. Whenever Doug was nearby, my stomach would churn. Even a year later, I was able to recount the conversations from that meeting verbatim and remember every single hurtful thing said. Eventually, after much hard work, and with help from others, he and I together compiled a list of "true facts" about that meeting. (Not my distorted version of the truth that I was bitterly clinging to.) I wrote that list down and kept it in my purse so I could review it when I was tempted to bitter or self-pitying thoughts. Some of the things on that list were: "We both misunderstood the purpose of the meeting" and "I hurt him deeply as well." I decided to make this an *Off-limits Area* in my mind. I would no longer revisit this event as I previously believed it to have occurred. Instead, I would read my list of truth over and over whenever I thought about the meeting. As time passed and God worked, I was able to see the truth about that time and my bitterness. I gave and received forgiveness. Now my memories of that meeting are so fuzzy that I can barely recall what was said. There are no hurtful remembrances of it at all. Praise God for His work in my heart and the reconciliation of this relationship! (Yesterday, Doug and I had a meeting. At the end, he gave me a hug. My stomach was just fine.)

Compile a list of God's promises on which to meditate. Hebrews 13:5 states that He will never leave us nor forsake us. 2 Corinthians 1:3-5 says He will comfort us. Philippians 1:6 promises that He will complete the work He's begun in us. 1 Peter 1:4 talks of our inheritance that will never perish, spoil, or fade. 2 Peter 1:3 says we have received everything we need in the Spirit for life and godliness. Ephesians 2:4 and following recounts God's amazing love and spiritual blessings for us. Make your own additions to this list and rehearse them regularly.

These days, I often give thanks for the wonderful husband God has gifted me with, for terrific kids, good health, a meaningful job, an amazing church, and many kind friends. Even better than those things, I have been saved from the wrath of God through Jesus' death on the cross. I have been made a child of the King and have been forgiven for every bitter thought and word I've ever uttered. I've received untold blessings from the hand of our gracious Father, and I will spend eternity singing around the throne. I will get to do what I love best at the feet of Jesus forever. I have a long list of blessings that overflow in praise and thanksgiving when I choose to count them. Ask God to give you truth to reflect on when you are tempted. Choose to be thankful rather than bitter.

Stay vigilant. Think about what you're thinking about. Keep track of the train of your thoughts and stop them when you find yourself wandering into bitter territory. Our brains operate out of habit. If your habit is to think angry and selfish thoughts, it will take great attention to change and repent of this. One of the fruits of the Holy Spirit is self-control. Ask for God's help, He promises to provide what we need to live a righteous life (2 Peter 1:3).

For example, if you find yourself thinking, "Jane has never liked/loved/respected/appreciated me," or "Bob never followed through on all his promises to me, it's so unfair," or "No one cares about me," or any other self-pitying thought, *stop!* Review what is true. Do not let your mind continue to dwell on these thoughts. Pray for self-control and selfless love. Ask Him to make your thoughts captive to Him and His truth.

I am in a carpooling season, so I spend many hours driving each week, which affords much idle time for my brain to work. Sometimes in the past, I would start off in a good mood, but by the time I reached my destination I would be furious with someone. Or I would be sad and in tears, thinking about my childhood. I was not controlling my thoughts. I allowed the enemy to plant a seed which grew without me even realizing it. It is much better to recite Scripture or sing a worship song. Pull your mind away from where it wants to go and fill it with truth.

Fill your mind with things that are true, lovely and worthy of praise (Philippians 4:8). Meditate on Christ, the gospel, the forgiveness you have received. Contemplate how much and how often God forgives you. Review what He's done for you, how He made a way for you to be forgiven. Use Scripture to remind yourself of God's great mercy and Christ's humility, how He suffered as though *He* was guilty even though He was the only one ever who didn't deserve punishment. Think of truths like:

> *God made him who had no sin to be sin for us, so that in him we might become the righteousness of God. (2 Corinthians 5:21 NIV)*

While we were still His enemies, God sent His Son Jesus to the cross so that we might be reconciled to Him. He paid our debt – wiped the slate clean. He gave us His righteousness and we are no longer condemned. (Romans 5:6-11; 8:1 NIV)

Contemplate the great love and mercy of God. Think about Jesus suffering on the cross to pay for your bitterness.

Choose thanksgiving. If one of the doorways to bitterness is self-pity, the remedy is to thank God for all His goodness and blessings. The self-pitying person may say, "I have nothing to be thankful for." That is because their usual practice is to focus on the selfish and the negative. But if you are a child of God, saved from His wrath and forgiven of your sins, you have much for which to be thankful. Start by thanking Him for your salvation. Then read through Psalms of thanksgiving and praise, and worship God for who He is. Then choose to find other things to be thankful for. It will take effort if you are not regularly in an "attitude of gratitude," but it must become your new habit if you want to overcome this temptation.

Recently I saw a news report where victims of a natural disaster were being interviewed. They had lost their homes and were scrambling just to gather the basic necessities of life. One woman complained that no one was helping them. They couldn't get any response from the local authorities – their situation was tragic and unfair. Another man threw up his hands and said, "Hey! We are still alive!" The woman complained about what she didn't have, and the man chose to give thanks for what he did.

One habit I've learned is to go through the alphabet giving thanks for one thing that starts with each letter. For example, *A—Lord, thank You that You are the Almighty One, who is in control of all things and I can trust and rely on You...B—Lord, thank You for the blood that was spilled for me on the cross that washes me clean...C—Thank You for this car that I am driving that is comfortable and reliable...*and so on (fudging if you need to on *X* and *Z*). Sometimes your mind will be drawn to spiritual blessings and sometimes to the more practical. For instance, "B" often provokes me to be thankful for the beauty that I'm surrounded with here in Colorado. Sometimes the letter will bring to mind someone's first name, and you can be thankful for them and then pray for them. What you're thankful for may change, but the habit you have started to develop will change your thinking.

#9 Be patient. Unless God chooses to perform an extraordinary miracle in your life, this will be a slow process. It will take time for your mind and heart to respond differently than they used to. It will take time for you to form new mental habits, fighting in the Spirit's power, and choosing gratitude. You may have to confess, repent, and forgive over and over. Don't be discouraged, your perseverance will bear fruit.

A dear friend told me that in the struggle to forgive a family member, she prayed diligently for an entire year before seeing her bitterness dissipate. That was such a huge encouragement to me when I was going through this. I would guess that it was several months before I started to feel released from the bondage of my bitterness. The whole process was at least a year and is still ongoing. There are days even now when I'm tempted back to the same old thinking. But by the grace of God and in the power of the Spirit, I fight it. He is still working in me, and His promises are still true.

15

Common Excuses (and the Truth That Sets You Free)

1. "I'm not bitter, I've just had so much pain and sorrow in my life. It's too much – it overflows! I can't help it."

We all experience tragedy and sorrow. If you haven't yet, you will. Later, we will explore godly responses to those situations, but for now I will just stress that God is the *Sovereign One,* the almighty King upon the throne. He rules the universe and controls every aspect of your life. All the hurts that have befallen you are in His plan and for His good purposes. Remember Romans 8:28: "And we know that in all things God works for the good of those who love him, who have been called according to his purpose" (NIV). This verse tells us there is purpose in our suffering.

God's purposes are often unclear to us, but we must trust that He has a good plan. In everything you suffer, God is working for your good and His glory. As verse 29 says, "For those God foreknew he also predestined to be conformed to the image of his Son." If you are God's child, He knew you before the world began and had a plan to conform you to the image of His Son Jesus. We don't know exactly what this plan looks like, but its purpose is to mold us and shape us, to chip away all the rough edges of our sin. Does it hurt sometimes? Yes! Yet God knows what He is doing, doesn't He? Another resounding yes! We are to trust our lives to Him and submit to His working, however painful it may be. In this sense, even "bad" things are good.

Remember, God is *for* you. He is on your side. Romans 5:3-4 says, "We rejoice in our sufferings, knowing that suffering produces endurance, and endurance produces character, and character produces hope (ESV)." God is not the disapproving, scowling Father some of us imagine Him to be. He is our loving *Abba* – Daddy – and He's right there in our corner. He wants us to grow up to be good kids, demonstrating maturity and holiness. He has promised to give us good things, including hope, and the power to fight sin and break free from the bondage of bitterness. He uses suffering to produce righteousness in our lives (Hebrews 12:11).

One of my favorite songs is *You Are For Me* sung by Kari Jobe. The lyrics say, in part:

> *You fill me*
> *You see me*
> *You know my every move*
> *And You love for me to sing to You*
> *And Lord I know that You are for me*

I know that You are for me
I know that You will never
Forsake me in my weakness

Pain is not an excuse to sin. Job, David, Joseph, and other significant biblical characters all suffered greatly as part of God's purpose for their lives. God did not even spare His own Son from pain. Jesus experienced rejection, humiliation, unfair accusations, torture, and death. But He trusted God and submitted to His plan without growing bitter or self-centered. Just because you are in pain and having struggles does not mean that God has abandoned you. It also does not make it acceptable to respond in ungodly ways.

I have a good friend who is a great mother. She is intensely interested in the lives of her children. She is loving and extremely affirming. She listens to them and asks questions. She models Christ to them, teaches them, and prays for them. But recently I was reminded that she did not have this kind of childhood or this kind of mother herself. Her parents divorced, forcing her to become independent and learn to do for herself. Yet, instead of becoming embittered over this, she chose the opposite path and became an interested, nurturing mother. She is a model of someone who didn't allow unhappy circumstances to drive her to self-pity or bitterness.

There was a time when I would have said that the greatest trial and pain in my life was my difficult relationship with Doug. The pain I suffered from feeling wronged by him was at times almost unbearable. And yet, because of that hard time, we now have an amazing story to tell of God's faithfulness. The book you are reading is a resultant blessing of that dark time. God knew the end of this story, and He had a plan to bring things together for our good and His glory. All praise goes to Him!

2. "I'm not bitter – I only have a short temper. This is just the way I am."

True, it *is* the way you are. You are a sinner like the rest of us. And some of us are more prone to anger and bitterness than others. That does not excuse it. The Bible says, "In your anger do not sin…and do not give the devil a foothold" (Ephesians 4:26-27 NIV). This means that anger can be the doorway to further sin, including bitterness. You must keep that door shut.

Proverbs warns that a "hot tempered [person] commits many sins" (Proverbs 29:22 NIV). James says, "Human anger does not produce the righteousness that God desires" (1:19-20 NIV). This should alert us to the urgency of repentance when we grow angry and upset.

3. "I'm not bitter, I'm demonstrating righteous anger."

The story of Jesus violently overturning tables in the temple is often used as an example. He was angry about the defilement of God's house and used a whip to drive out the moneychangers. Yes, there is a place for righteous anger, such as when we witness the abuse of those whom God has created in His own image or the defilement of things God has created to be sacred. But most of the time, people with a temper are reacting to offenses (or *perceived* offenses) against themselves, not protecting the rights or dignity of others. What they want to call *righteous* anger is usually an excuse to justify their *sinful and selfish* anger.

4. "I wouldn't be bitter if *he/she* didn't...."

This is the classic tale of bitterness—refusing to see my sin for what it is by placing blame on those who have hurt or wronged me. Maybe the other person really did sin against me. Still, my bitter reaction is sin against God. I will not stand in that other person's shoes at Judgment, I will stand in my own. *How did I react to being wronged or sinned against? Did I love? Did I show grace? Did I forgive?* That is what I should be thinking about, rather than accusing someone else of wrongdoing.

5. "If I forgive, I'm condoning what he/she did."

Not true! Forgiveness, by definition, assumes that wrong was done that needs forgiving. You are only saying that your response will be grace and love and compassion. When God forgives the awful sins we have committed against Him, is He condoning our sin? No! God hates sin. His grace does not endorse our offenses, it acknowledges they are real, then pardons them. That is what we should do with offenses against us.

6. "I'm not bitter, I just get hurt easily."

(This is my personal favorite.) I do not believe that being hurt equals being bitter, but what do we do with that hurt? Do we wallow in self-pity? Do we nurse it and soothe it? Do we tell others about it? Who are we concerned about? Ourselves, right? This puts us in grave danger of becoming bitter.

Let's examine some common ways we often feel hurt:

- *I have an idea, but you reject it.*

- *I say "Hello," but you turn away.*

- *I contact you often, but you never initiate contact with me.*

- *You spend time with others but not with me.*

- *I do kind things for you but receive no gratitude (or not enough).*

- *I have talents, but you do not appreciate them or ask me to use them.*

I'm sure you can think of many other scenarios, but essentially they all boil down to one thing—*I'm not getting what I want.* "Me," "my," and "I," are the pertinent terms here. Hurt comes from selfishness.

Getting your feelings hurt is a selfish reaction that can quickly lead to anger and bitterness. I don't say this lightly. I struggle with hurt feelings quite often. This has led to much of the bitterness in my life. I don't think it's the initial reaction that is sinful but what we do with it. I have tried to compare it to a man's struggle against lust. If a beautiful woman walks by wearing next to nothing, he will look. It's the natural reaction. But what he does in the next few seconds determines whether he will succumb to lust (looking again, starting to imagine, etc.) or resist the temptation by purposefully placing his thoughts elsewhere. If you are susceptible to hurt, you may not be able to prevent having that initial feeling of *ouch!* But what you do in the next few minutes will determine whether you sink into sin or not. If you move toward self-pity, your hurt feelings will be magnified by thinking how unfair it all is, how you can never win, and how no one has ever really loved you. Then perhaps you will feel anger for the slight you've suffered or the injustice that has been done. You start to rant internally about that person or situation, and there you go...off to bitterness.

You must speak truth to yourself. Give yourself a mental shake and fight off this train of thought. Replace the thoughts of self-pity with thoughts of thanksgiving. Bury those hurts under love. Pray for the person who hurt you, and pray for yourself. Ask the Lord for wisdom, self-control, and an abundance of love and patience. Choose to put your mind somewhere else. Put on the armor of God and stand firm. Recite Scripture or sing a worship song. Strive against sin.

Depending on the situation, it sometimes takes me a day or so to go through this process and not allow the hurt to stick. But I have found that as I fight hurt feelings, I have them less and less.

And God will help. He knows we are weak, and He helps us when we ask. He will give us the power to fight the hurt feelings and overcome selfishness:

As a father shows compassion to his children,
so the Lord shows compassion to those who fear him.
For he knows our frame;
he remembers that we are dust.
(Psalm 103:13-14 ESV)

And just as a reminder, selfishness is *bad*. The Bible calls it part of worldly wisdom that is demonic (James 3:14-16 NIV). The world says, "Look out for number one," "Treat yourself well because you're worth it," and "You deserve to be happy." We must not fall prey to these lies. Our "number one" needs to be Christ. We don't deserve to be treated well or to be happy, we deserve God's punishment because of our sin. Only through God's grace have we become His beloved children. And there is no room for selfish bitterness in those who have received such kindness from God.

James explains why we fight with others. He says it is because things don't go our way. Other people, including *God*, don't give us what we want, so we get mad:

> *What causes fights and quarrels among you? Don't they come from your desires that battle within you? You desire but do not have, so you kill. You covet but you cannot get what you want, so you quarrel and fight. You do not have because you do not ask God. When you ask, you do not receive, because you ask with wrong motives, that you may spend what you get on your pleasures. (James 4:1-3 NIV)*

To give a fairly trivial example, if a friend chooses not to sit with me at an event, I may feel hurt, believing that she didn't like me enough to sit with me and seems to prefer others over me. (Yes, this is very "junior high," but it's reality for some of us.) I am being selfish and assuming the worst of my friend.

If I continue down this path, I will treat her as my enemy. If I want to walk a different path, the righteous path, I have two choices: 1) cover the (perceived) offense with love, or 2) talk to her about it. If I say, "Hey, I thought you were going to sit by me?" she may say, "Oh sorry, I didn't see you," or "Oh, I forgot." Or maybe there was someone she particularly needed to talk to. If I speak to her, I must accept her apology or explanation. If I don't, I will start down a dangerous path.

What if someone I desire a friendship with repeatedly rebuffs my attempts to get together? Will I feel hurt? Yes! Why? Because I desire to be loved and wanted by others. I think we have some things in common and could have a nice friendship. What should I do about it? Ask the Lord to give me wisdom and love in this situation. The sad truth may be that this person does not desire a closer relationship with me. In that case, I need to continue to love her and guard my heart against anger and bitterness. The truth may only be that she does not have room on her calendar right now to cultivate another friendship. Or maybe she does not notice my attempts to establish or deepen our friendship. If I am brave, I might speak frankly to her with a gentle and loving spirit. But what I must not do is descend into self-pity or transfer this hurt to others. ("Obviously *no one* wants to be my friend since *she* didn't.")

What if I am hurt because someone's gifting is greater than mine and they get the spotlight? What if I am not asked to teach (or sing, or preach, or lead, etc.)? First I must examine my motives. I am hurt because I am jealous and because I want to be the most liked, the most desired, the most sought-after person. Selfish? Sinful? Yes! Love would say "I want what is best for the ministry or organization, whether that person is me or someone else." Perhaps I am gifted and need to work on and develop my gifts, but I must not be jealous of or bitter against those who are currently in leadership.

Sometimes, people are unkind with their words, maybe by speaking carelessly or trying to be funny. In these situations, we must have a forgiving heart ready to cover these offenses with love. We may also speak gently but truthfully to them about it, as long as our goal is reconciliation and unity.

In *How to Be Free From Bitterness*, Heather Wilson Torosyan's essay addresses the subject of hurt feelings. She suggests we ask ourselves: "Do I have a *right* to be hurt? Must I remain susceptible to hurt feelings until everybody else is perfect?" She then concludes: "We would like to have people so nice to us all the time that there would never be an occasion for us to be hurt. Obviously this is unrealistic..." (p. 49).

If we look to the example of Jesus in our interpersonal relationships, we will model humility. We won't insist on having things our way, we will seek to love and serve others. The Bible tells us how Jesus—who is God and does have the right to be exalted—laid down His rights and became obedient to the will of the Father.

Paul tells us:

> *Do nothing out of selfish ambition or vain conceit. Rather, in humility value others above yourselves, not looking to your own interests but each of you to the interests of the others. In your relationships with one another, have the same mindset*

as Christ Jesus: Who, being in very nature God, did not consider equality with God something to be used to his own advantage; rather, he made himself nothing by taking the very nature of a servant, being made in human likeness. And being found in appearance as a man, he humbled himself by becoming obedient to death—even death on a cross! (Philippians 2:3-8 NIV)

Finally, Torosyan summarizes, "When we feel hurt, it is because there is no ready forgiveness in our hearts...for every temptation the Lord provides a way of escape, there is no reason why any of us should ever be hurt again" (p. 51).

A page from my story:

After repenting of my bitterness toward Doug and becoming free from the tangled mess, I began to ask myself, *Why had I been bitter? What sin did he really commit against me?* The answer was surprising. He didn't sin against me at all. (This is an important point: bitterness is a response to the perceived sins of others as well as actual sins.) My bitterness started because my feelings were hurt. I had expectations that he did not fulfill. He didn't act the way I thought he should. He didn't do things the way I wanted him to, the way I had suggested. He failed to implement my ideas. He didn't praise my talents. He didn't seem to appreciate all my efforts. He just didn't seem to like me very much. My feelings were hurt over and over, and then I began to consistently feel wronged. I decided that he did not like, respect, or appreciate me.

It is so unfair...I do so much. (Self-pity creeps in.) Over time, these beliefs became firmly cemented in my mind, and I could see no other reality. Everything he did or said was because he didn't like me, respect me, or appreciate me. I became angry easily, always drawing the worst possible conclusion from his words and actions. I was offended when he teased me or made a little joke at my expense, seeing it as evidence of his lack of respect for me. Anything kind he said or did was disregarded. I created a false picture of him in my mind, but neither he nor anyone else could convince me that it was false. I was firm in my convictions. Only the Holy Spirit could soften my heart under these circumstances. And praise God, He did!

16

How to Respond When God's Hand Is Hard

Bitterness often follows tragedy. Divorce by a spouse or betrayal by a friend can be a great temptation. The death of a loved one often leads to anger against God. The death of a child often spells the end of a marriage as grief and resentment (especially toward God) provoke other sins culminating in irreparable damage to the relationship.

In the Old Testament, David's loyal men almost stoned him to death when their wives and children were captured and taken away. They were devastated and despaired of ever seeing them again. They blamed David. It almost destroyed them all (1 Samuel 30:5-6).

RESPONDING WELL

Many circumstances are beyond our control: when a loved one is diagnosed with cancer or develops a terrible illness, or when you are in a serious accident, or when the market crashes and you are financially ruined, or when your child dies suddenly, or when your house burns to the ground. How do you react? How *should* you react?

Let's look at the story of Job. In chapter 1, he learned that his children were dead, his property had been destroyed, and all of his riches were stolen. How did he respond?

> *Then Job arose and tore his robe and shaved his head and fell on the ground and worshiped. And he said, "Naked I came from my mother's womb, and naked shall I return. The Lord gave, and the Lord has taken away; blessed be the name of the Lord." In all this Job did not sin or charge God with wrong. (Job 1:20-22 ESV)*

The key is, "Job did not sin or charge God with wrong." Worshipping God and blessing His name amidst trouble is a good first response to have.

In chapter 2, his health was taken away, adding physical affliction to the crushing grief and emotional pain he was already experiencing. Then his wife turned on him, suggesting that he "curse God and die."

His reply? "You are talking like a foolish woman. Shall we accept good from God, and not trouble?" (Job 2:10 NIV)

And once again we are told, "In all this, Job did not sin in what he said." (Job 2:10 NIV)

Job called his wife "foolish," or other translations say, "godless fool." In other words, to talk this way is to have a godless worldview, a way of looking at life that does not take into account God's plan and control over all things. Mrs. Job interpreted their situation without remembering God's sovereignty. She did not trust that God was working out His perfect plan. She focused only on the immediate, temporal, painful circumstances.

Isn't that what we so often do in hard times?

RESPONDING SINFULLY

Eventually, Job, too, took his eyes off of God and put them on his circumstances. As grief and pain overwhelmed him, he responded poorly. He complained and wallowed in self-pity:

> *Therefore I will not restrain my mouth; I will speak in the anguish of my spirit; I will complain in the bitterness of my soul. How long will You not look away from me, nor leave me alone till I swallow my spit? (Job 7:11, 19 ESV)*

He charged God with being unfair:

> *For he crushes me with a tempest and multiplies my wounds without cause; he will not let me get my breath, but fills me with bitterness. (Job 9:17-18 ESV)*

He trumpeted his own righteousness while doubting God's:

> *I have not departed from the commandment of his lips; I have treasured the words of his mouth more than my portion*

of food. But he is unchangeable, and who can turn him back? What he desires, that he does. (Job 23:12-13 ESV)

He disparaged God as harsh and uncaring:

God has cast me into the mire, and I have become like dust and ashes. I cry to you for help and you do not answer me; I stand, and you only look at me. You have turned cruel to me; with the might of your hand you persecute me. (Job 30:19-21 ESV)

Had Job fallen into sin?

Let's review: he wallows in self-pity, accuses God of being unfair and unkind, speaks self-righteously, denies any fault on his part, and again swims in oceans of self-pity. This sure sounds like bitterness. But the clearest answer comes when the Lord rebuked him. If there was no sin to point out, there would have been no reason for God's strong words.

REPENTANCE

In chapter 38, the Lord spoke to Job from a tornado. (Imagine the voice of God coming to you from that kind of powerful force. That would surely get my attention!) His message was basically, "Who are you, Job, to talk back to me and to question me? Are you more powerful than I am? Are you the King of creation? Did you set the world in place?"

We do not know what is going on in the heavenly realms, and we cannot always see what God's overarching plan is.

But we do know that no purpose of the Almighty One can be thwarted. He is the King of the universe. And He is working all things for our good (Romans 8:28). Why would we want to change His plan, even if we could? We do not know better than He. Our choices might be easier for ourselves, but they would not be better. He is wise and good, faithful and true, all-powerful and all-knowing. Whatever He chooses to do is the very best choice, even when it hurts. Our place is to submit ourselves to God and worship Him, even during disastrous times. He is God, we are not. He is the Creator, we are the creatures. He is the Lord, we are His servants.

After the tornado, Job got it. He recognized his sin. He realized that he was out of line in accusing God. He humbly repented:

> *I know that you can do all things, and that no purpose of yours can be thwarted...Therefore I have uttered what I did not understand, things too wonderful for me, which I did not know...I had heard of you by the hearing of the ear, but now my eye sees you; therefore I despise myself, and repent in dust and ashes." (Job 42:1, 3, 5, 6 ESV)*

God forgave Job and then blessed him abundantly, even more in the latter part of his life than the first. I find this astonishing, especially since Job was so prosperous before all this calamity occurred (Job 42:15-16). I believe Job died a happy man. This should greatly encourage us, especially if we have been guilty of bitterness against God. He will forgive and bless if we come to Him in sincere repentance. Bitterness does not have to be the end of our story.

But this story also contains a warning. Job, a righteous man, who responded well at first, eventually slid into bitterness. If calamity has been part of your life, be on guard. Even if you have responded well initially, you must remain vigilant. You must guard your heart.

SWEAT THE SMALL STUFF

Even little disappointments can trigger a tragic response if you are not careful.

As I write this, I am suffering a big letdown. Something I was greatly looking forward to doing next weekend has fallen through. It's not anyone's fault, the circumstances are beyond anyone's control. There is no one I can blame for this. Still, I feel very sad. What do I do with this crushing disappointment? My first temptation is self-pity: *Poor me, I never get to do anything fun.* The next temptation is resentment toward God: *Why doesn't anything ever work out for me, Lord? You could have kept this from happening. Don't You care about me?*

Please understand, this would not be a big deal to anyone else. It's just something I really wanted to do, and now it's not going to happen. But maybe you can identify with this kind of situation better than with Job's string of disasters. Disappointments are much more common in our lives than the big calamities, but our response needs to be the same. I need to make the decision right now to submit to God, to ask His forgiveness for my wanderings into self-pity, and to turn my mind elsewhere. I'm going to do my work, choose to be thankful, fill my mind with truth in Scripture and song lyrics. (And it worked, the Lord gave me victory and peace. The rest of that day was not colored by that disappointment.)

When God allows tragedy, we are to worship Him, submit to Him, and ask for strength to endure. It is sin to complain or accuse God of unfairness, wrongdoing, or negligence. We must not focus on ourselves, wallow in self-pity, or long for the former days. Instead, we must be thankful, content, and faithful to Jesus.

17

How to Respond When Others Hurt Us

We are all sinners. We all sin against God and each other. This means you have been hurt by others. It's a common human ailment. Examples are betrayal, infidelity, abuse, slander, wrongful loss of employment, theft, and other terrible ways in which people harm us. Our tendency is to think we deserve better and to want restitution and revenge. But what kind of reaction does God want from us?

CONSIDER JOSEPH

Joseph's brothers were jealous of him, so they plotted to kill him. But they decided against this and sold him into slavery instead. Now, he was no picnic to live with, and he certainly provoked his brothers, but undoubtedly he was the wronged party in this story.

When they met again years later, the tables were turned.

He had risen to the second in command over the entire Egyptian empire. Pharaoh had given him authority over the whole kingdom. One might expect that when his brothers came to see him, he would be angry and treat them poorly. Surely we could expect him to desire vengeance. But he didn't. He had trusted God through all the malice shown to him by others. He trusted the grand plan of a good God. He realized that their sin was part of God's purpose for him. He said to them, "It was not you who sent me here but God" (Genesis 45:8 ESV). This wasn't simplistic optimism or naiveté. He knew that his brothers had intended to harm him, but there was another perspective. God had a plan. So rather than becoming vengeful, he simply said, "As for you, you meant evil against me, but God meant it for good" (Genesis 50:20 ESV).

If we have our eyes firmly focused on serving Jesus, we will not worry about how others treat us. We won't respond with bitterness or plot revenge against them. We will remember Who is in our corner. ("The Lord is on my side; I will not fear. What can man do to me?" Psalm 118:6 ESV)

CONSIDER PAUL

Paul is another good example of one who suffered greatly at the hands of his fellow man. Everywhere he went, he was beaten or jailed or otherwise persecuted. His crime? Preaching the gospel and serving the church, doing what God had called him to do. How did he respond? Certainly a little self-pity would have seemed reasonable. He could have complained to God and asked for a lightning bolt from Heaven in judgment. Instead, he left the punishing to God (Romans 12:19) and trusted Him to do what was best.

Even when some of his fellow believers abandoned him, he responded with grace and forgiveness:

> *Alexander the metalworker did me a great deal of harm. The Lord will repay him for what he has done. You too should be on your guard against him, because he strongly opposed our message. At my first defense, no one came to my support, but everyone deserted me. May it not be held against them. (2 Timothy 2:14-16 NIV)*

In 2 Corinthians 11:23-27, Paul spoke of being whipped, stoned, jailed, and shipwrecked. He had also been regularly threatened with harm by both Jews and Gentiles. And he experienced extreme cold, hunger, and nakedness. Yet notice his attitude through all of these disastrous circumstances:

> *To this very hour we go hungry and thirsty, we are in rags, we are brutally treated, we are homeless. We work hard with our own hands. When we are cursed, we bless; when we are persecuted, we endure it; when we are slandered, we answer kindly. We have become the scum of the earth, the garbage of the world—right up to this moment. (1 Corinthians 4:11-13 NIV)*

Instead of becoming cantankerous and sour toward people,

he exhorted his fellow believers to grace, forgiveness, and
unselfish love:

> *Make allowance for each other's faults, and forgive anyone
> who offends you. Remember, the Lord forgave you, so you
> must forgive others. (Colossians 3:13 NLT)*

> *For the entire law is fulfilled in keeping this one command:
> "Love your neighbor as yourself." (Galatians 5:14 NIV)*

But most of all, Paul's perspective on who he was and his
role in serving Christ enabled him to endure harsh treatment
without becoming self-pitying or bitter. Who was he? A man
who had been forgiven much. What was his role? To proclaim Christ to the Gentiles (Philippians 1:16-18). He kept his
eyes focused on the task of preaching the gospel. Everything
else became secondary, even his own comfort and safety. He
would endure anything for the sake of Christ. There was no
room in his mind for selfishness, taking offense, or blaming
God for hardships.

> *And because I preach this Good News, I am suffering and
> have been chained like a criminal. But the word of God
> cannot be chained. So I am willing to endure anything if it
> will bring salvation and eternal glory in Christ Jesus to those
> God has chosen. (2 Timothy 2:9-10 NLT)*

> *For the sake of Christ, then, I am content with weaknesses,
> insults, hardships, persecutions, and calamities. For when I
> am weak, then I am strong. (2 Corinthians 12:10 ESV)*

How do you respond to injustice or unfair treatment? How do I? Do we follow Paul's example and commitment to Christ? Do we serve Him by loving others regardless of what they do to us? Is extending forgiveness more important than personal pain or comfort?

LOVE COVERS ALL

In his book *Respectable Sins*, Jerry Bridges offers two solutions for overcoming anger and the bitterness it will lead to. He says, "First, we must always look to the Sovereignty of God. God doesn't cause people to sin against us, but He does allow it, and it is always allowed for a purpose — most often our own growth in Christlikeness...Second, we should pray that God will enable us to grow in love. In 1 Peter...Peter keeps emphasizing the importance of brotherly love — that is love toward fellow believers. For example, he writes, 'Above all, keep loving one another earnestly, since love covers a multitude of sins' (1 Peter 4:8)" (pp. 133-134).

I believe 1 Peter 4:8 is a key verse to meditate on in overcoming the sin of bitterness. Remember, the remedy to bitterness is love. We must let love cover over the sins of others toward us. If I demonstrate love toward you, I am going to choose to ignore that insult or careless word you uttered. I will show you grace and give you the benefit of the doubt. I will bury or disregard your sin against me. That's what love does, it keeps no record of wrongs (1 Corinthians 13:4).

There is a place for confronting a brother or sister who sins against you, maybe even with an elder or trusted friend to mediate, but you must be careful that your motives are reconciliation, not revenge. I heard a story of a woman who was summoned to her pastor's office one evening without knowing why. There she was confronted with an angry woman who was prepared to accuse her with a long list of grievances. The accuser felt she was doing it according to scriptural principles because she had involved the pastor. However, her motive was to berate the unsuspecting woman, not to promote love and unity. You can imagine the outcome of that meeting wasn't altogether favorable.

If your motive is truly Christ-honoring, you will only confront as a means to resolution and peace between the two of you. And you will speak to the other person kindly and accordingly. Perhaps the person is unaware of what they are doing, and by gently having it pointed out, they will repent and your relationship will be restored.

I think the biggest caution in this scenario is that the person being confronted must be assured of your motives. If you say, "I desire to have a relationship with you, and here is something that is troubling me. Please consider this…," they are far more likely to listen than if you say, "You are sinning. Here is what Scripture says about your sin." If they do not repent, or if they refuse to listen, then you need to involve others, but your goal is still to be reconciliation and unity. Sometimes it is not possible to achieve that, but do everything in *your* power. Romans 12:18 says that we should do whatever we can to be at peace with everyone. We cannot control other people's behavior, but we can control ourselves. If the other person chooses not to respond, we must let them. And we must love them still.

Here is a fictional scenario based on real stories: Imagine a girl who loved Jesus and desired to serve Him with her whole heart. She wanted to be a missionary, so she went to a Christian college. There she studied hard and met a wonderful, like-minded man who was also headed for the mission field. They married soon after graduation with great dreams of serving the Lord together in foreign lands. While they were paying off debt and serving in the local church to prepare for their work overseas, he got involved with some ungodly friends. He began partying with them after work, often staying out late and coming home drunk. One bad habit led to another, and a few years later our good girl who had done everything right found herself in a mess. She had two small children to care for and her dream of overseas ministry had been shattered. Her husband was addicted to alcohol, unfaithful to her, and even abusive at times. She had no choice but to leave him.

This is a tragic situation in every way, and this poor young woman has been terribly wronged. But how will she respond? What will she do with the rest of her days?

Terrible stories like this (or worse) are real. Many times people find themselves in situations not of their own making. What can this poor woman do? Believe God. Trust God. He promises that He is going to work things out for her good (Romans 8:28) and His glory. She needs to focus on what she is immediately called to do—raise her children to love and serve Jesus, and cultivate a heart of thankfulness even in the midst of these hard times—then see how the Lord leads beyond that, and always with her guard up against selfishness and hatred. Perhaps the Lord will use her story to encourage others. Perhaps He has another ministry for her working with abandoned or abused women. God is still our loving, sovereign Father, no matter what our circumstances are, and His plans are for our good.

The righteous way to respond when someone offends you can be summed up in one word—*forgive:* "Be kind to one another, tender-hearted, forgiving one another, as God in Christ forgave you" (Ephesians 4:32 ESV).

The definition of tenderhearted includes the terms *kind, gentle,* and *sentimental.* Sentimental can carry a somewhat negative connotation. It can mean someone who cries in a movie when the puppy can't find its way home, or someone who's a pushover or always dreaming of the past. I don't think those are the characteristics intended to be portrayed in this verse. I think a better definition would be *soft.* This is someone who responds gently in a tough situation, someone who responds with pity when confronted with anger, someone who responds softly even when treated harshly, someone who asks, "Is something else the matter? Did I do something to offend you? What's going on?"

Another word we might use is *compassionate.* Compassion involves sympathy and concern for others. A compassionate woman will contact a sister who is struggling and offer encouragement or bring a meal. A compassionate friend will visit a friend in the hospital while they are sitting with their dying parent. It means "to suffer with." This is especially appropriate in this context. Jesus suffered for us on the cross and empathizes with us now. That is how we should act toward people who offend us. We should be kind, soft, and forgiving like Jesus is toward us.

18

About Forgiveness

Forgiveness means to cancel or release the wrong done to us by someone. You no longer hold it against them. You no longer put it to their account. You no longer want them to be found out and paid back. You don't "remember" the offense anymore. If the thought pops up, you consciously put it away and don't rehearse it. It doesn't matter if the offender is contrite or apologizes. If you truly forgive, then the offense is not sitting on their record. The debt is wiped clean. You don't bring it up, count it against them, or purposely think upon it. If they offend again, it is not added to an existing pile of offenses, it is just one new offense. You extend grace to the offender and offer them the benefit of the doubt. Forgiveness has a poor memory while bitterness remembers every detail.

Steven R. Tracy, in his book *Mending the Soul* says:

> "Forgiveness is letting go of my right to hurt another person for hurting me...By letting go of my right to

take personal revenge on my abuser, I am relinquishing the roles of judge, jury, and executioner over to God…Forgiveness is an act of faith, for when one forgives, he or she is trusting that God can and will bring judgment and create justice for all the wrongs committed against him or her. By faith we let go of our attempts to exact revenge from abusers, trusting that God will carry out precisely the right inescapable vengeance that justice requires" (pp. 186-187).

He goes on to say:

"One of the Greek terms used for human forgiveness in the New Testament is [*charizomai*] (2 Corinthians 2:7, 10; 12:13; Ephesians 4:32; Colossians 3:13), which means to extend grace…it means—based on the mercy and grace of God I have experienced—I'm willing to extend kindness even to my enemies (Matthew 5:43-47), with a view toward their own repentance and healing" (p. 187).

WHY DO I NEED TO REPENT OF BITTERNESS AND FORGIVE OTHERS?

The first reason is because you desire to please God. God hates sin. He killed His own Son to pay its penalty. We should not take this lightly. Sin separates us from God, and those who persist in sin do not have fellowship with Him.

Christians are called to show grace and forgiveness:

Don't repay evil for evil. Don't retaliate with insults when people insult you. Instead, pay them back with a blessing.

*That is what God has called you to do, and he will bless you
for it. (1 Peter 3:9 NLT)*

Also, Jesus teaches that loving our enemies is a validation of
our identity as God's children:

*I say, love your enemies! Pray for those who persecute
you! In that way, you will be acting as true children of your
Father in Heaven. For he gives his sunlight to both the evil
and the good, and he sends rain on the just and the unjust
alike. If you love only those who love you, what reward is
there for that? Even corrupt tax collectors do that much. If
you are kind only to your friends, how are you different from
anyone else? Even pagans do that. (Matthew 5:44-47 NLT)*

Secondly, our sin affects others whether we realize it or
not. We have a greater sphere of influence than we often
know. Those in your family, your workplace, and your
church will be affected by your sin even if you try to keep it
hidden. Do you want to teach your children or grandchildren
to respond bitterly to the offenses against them? My fervent
desire is that my children will not grow up struggling with
bitterness. After all the mistakes I've made, I want to model
a forgiving and loving life to them and help them overcome
this temptation. What about your friends at work or your
church family? Do you want to influence them by your bad
example? Bitterness is a root that grows up and defiles many.
(Think of baby aspens popping up all over the yard....)

And lastly, you will have joy and freedom if you repent

of bitterness and forgive those who have offended you. I said earlier that wallowing in bitterness will depress your spirit and place a heavy burden on your shoulders. Once this burden is lifted, you will feel light and free. The pain will be greatly reduced, perhaps even totally wiped away. Much of my pain occurred because I felt wronged. I felt that I must be vindicated, that someone should defend me and help me. I focused on myself, my hurts, my sorrow. But focusing on and loving others produces joy and happiness. Obedience brings joy! This is a wonderful feeling, standing in stark contrast to the heaviness we feel when we are embittered.

HOW FAR SHOULD FORGIVENESS GO?

I think one of the hardest things about forgiving others is that they don't just offend us once. It usually happens over and over. The Bible speaks to this:

> *Then Peter came to Jesus and asked, "Lord, how many times shall I forgive my brother or sister who sins against me? Up to seven times?" Jesus answered, "I tell you, not seven times, but seventy times seven." (Matthew 18:21-22 NIV)*

> *"If another believer sins, rebuke that person; then if there is repentance, forgive. Even if that person wrongs you seven times a day and each time turns again and asks forgiveness, you must forgive." (Luke 17:3-4 NLT)*

What if a person sins against you seven times per day, 365 days a year for 80 years? That's 204,400 times you must forgive! It's not just 70 x 7 = 490. The point isn't that we should specifically count how many times we are to forgive. The point is that we are to forgive over and over and over. There is never a time when we may say, "I've forgiven them enough times, now I'm done. I've fulfilled the quota." Jesus means that we must forgive continually, unendingly, and completely.

WHAT IF I JUST CAN'T FORGIVE?

You might think that you are a special case. You simply cannot forgive, especially because of what they have done and how often they have done it. You have suffered so much that forgiveness is simply impossible. Furthermore, they show no remorse. They don't even believe they are doing wrong. They certainly don't deserve your forgiveness. Or you might say, "I will forgive them, but I will never forget!" which may not be forgiveness at all.

The forgiveness we are talking about starts with God. He forgives us—men and women who have offended Him deeply and more consistently than any harm done from one human being to another. On top of that, we continue to sin even after we have experienced His grace. Surely, He would have the right to say, "That's it! I'm done with all of you. You have reached the limit." But He doesn't. He continues to forgive. And the more we see the greatness of our sin against Him and the vastness of His forgiveness toward us, the easier it is to let go of our claims on others.

Consider the parable of the unforgiving servant:

"Therefore, the kingdom of Heaven is like a king who

wanted to settle accounts with his servants. As he began the settlement, a man who owed him ten thousand bags of gold [about $520,000] was brought to him. Since he was not able to pay, the master ordered that he and his wife and his children and all that he had be sold to repay the debt. At this the servant fell on his knees before him. 'Be patient with me,' he begged, 'and I will pay back everything.' The servant's master took pity on him, canceled the debt and let him go. But when that servant went out, he found one of his fellow servants who owed him a hundred silver coins [about $100]. He grabbed him and began to choke him. 'Pay back what you owe me!' he demanded. His fellow servant fell to his knees and begged him, 'Be patient with me, and I will pay it back.' But he refused. Instead, he went off and had the man thrown into prison until he could pay the debt. When the other servants saw what had happened, they were outraged and went and told their master everything that had happened. Then the master called the servant in. 'You wicked servant,' he said, 'I canceled all that debt of yours because you begged me to. Shouldn't you have had mercy on your fellow servant just as I had on you?' In anger his master handed him over to the jailers to be tortured, until he should pay back all he owed. This is how my Heavenly Father will treat each of you unless you forgive your brother or sister from your heart." (Matthew 18:23-35)

Jesus said God will not forgive those who will not forgive others. A sober warning indeed.

But even with this warning, it sometimes seems too difficult. How can we do it?

God has given us everything we need to live a godly life

(2 Peter 1:3-4). Everything, even a forgiving heart. It's a promise. We do not have to wallow in the selfishness of bitterness and unforgiveness. We are not trapped in our sinful nature. We have power through the Holy Spirit. The same mighty power that raised Christ from the dead indwells believers (Ephesians 1:19-20). This power can make a dead man come alive. This power can make blind eyes see, and soften hearts of stone. A bitter, selfish person can be transformed into a loving one. Christians have the power and ability to forgive.

All things exist to bring glory and pleasure to Jesus (Colossians 1:16-18). For you to persist in sin does not bring glory to Christ. You are in a cosmic battle and must decide whose side you are on. If you are obedient to Him, He will work in amazing ways and bring glory to Himself through your circumstances, even the hard ones. Remember the story of Corrie ten Boom? She was imprisoned in a Nazi concentration camp where her beloved sister died. Years later, she met one of her former prison guards and was faced with a tough choice. Would she forgive? Could she? With the Lord's help, she did forgive that man, and she experienced great freedom and joy.

What if you say, "I just can't change the way I feel?" Maybe you can't do that at first, but you can change the way you *think*. If you do this, it will eventually change your feelings. If you are a follower of Jesus Christ, you have the Holy Spirit and in Him, everything you need for living a righteous, godly life.

So, how did I do it?

This is not something we just muster up on our own. We need the power of the Holy Spirit to even take the first steps. In my case, it started with a choice, a *declaration to forgive*: "Lord, I choose to forgive Bill for what he's done (and name it specifically). You know he does not deserve forgiveness, just as I do not deserve to be forgiven by You. Lord, I want to do this in obedience to You, so please give me the ability. Help me! I choose to forgive Bill. I will not hold on to this or put it against his account any longer. Lord, help me to do this."

Repeat your own version of this prayer again and again.

The first time you pray, you may feel like you're just reciting words and don't actually mean it. But God *will* answer. He *will* work. He *will* change you if you ask Him to. I know this from experience. I have seen it happen in my own heart and mind.

Then pray for Bill's salvation, or sanctification if he is a believer. Pray for Bill's family and his work. Pray for Bill in any way you can think of. Pray that your love toward Bill will increase.

The next day, when something else that Bill has done comes to your mind, pray it again. Pray it several times throughout the day if you need to. Then pray it again the next day, and the next day, and the next. Ask God for power, for love toward Bill, for His Spirit to work in your heart to soften it. He promises to do it!

I've said earlier that often the objects of our bitterness are people close to us or regularly involved in our lives. So what happens the next time you see or talk to Bill and he's not very nice? Pray it again! "Lord, I choose to forgive Bill. You forgave me when I didn't deserve it, and I'm going to forgive Him now with the Spirit's power." Pay attention to what you're thinking, fight with the armor of God protecting your mind and your heart. Then watch how God works!

TRUE FORGIVENESS

How can I tell if I have truly forgiven you and am no longer bitter?

1. You see your own sin in the relationship.

> **Admission of fault and acknowledgment of failure is the fruit of a life that's been set free. ~ Tullian Tchividjian**

Since bitterness is such a blame game, and we so commonly excuse it in ourselves, to be convicted of your own sin is clear evidence of God's Spirit working in you. If you can point to a past conflict and see that you were sinfully contributing to the situation, praise God! Your eyes have been opened.

2. You don't remember every detail of hurtful conversations or events.

When you are freed from the bondage of bitterness, you will experience new and blessed forgetfulness. You will not "remember" all those offenses against you. Those chains will not bind you any longer. I put *remember* in quotes because it's not as though your memory actually has been erased, but your habits of thinking have changed. By the mighty power of God, you have stopped dwelling on those things. You don't *remember* them against anyone else. They no longer torment you or hurt you. You are free!

3. You desire to have a relationship with them (if possible and appropriate).

In some cases, it may not be feasible or wise. Maybe your bitterness was toward someone no longer living or a person with whom you really should not reestablish contact. Or maybe they will refuse to reconcile or reestablish a relationship. In those situations, as far as it depends on *you*, be at peace with them (Romans 12:18), and don't cause more strife pushing your way in. If your heart is truly willing and humble, that is all you can do. Their response is out of your control.

I want to comment on reconciliation here. Forgiveness does not automatically equal reconciliation. Some of the consequences of sin break trust and take time to rebuild. Many times bitterness exists on both sides of a relationship, and even if one person seeks forgiveness and healing, the other may not choose to reciprocate. I am immensely thankful for my dear boss and pastor Doug. He forgave me immediately once I realized and repented of my sin. His desire had been reconciliation since the beginning of our struggles, and he has made efforts to foster a good relationship with me. He continues to work hard at being a friend. I can't say enough about what overwhelming evidence there is of the Spirit's working in him and through him.

4. You wish for (and pray for) their success and blessing.

You no longer desire revenge, but rather to see them flourish and prosper. If the person is a believer, you pray that God will bless them. If an unbeliever, you pray for their salvation. When you hear about their successes, you rejoice. When you hear about their misfortunes, you grieve and try to help in any way you can. Your heart's desire for them is genuine happiness.

5. You speak well of them to others.

This is applicable even if they are long dead. If you are done with bitterness, whenever the person comes up in conversation, your desire is to enhance their image in the eyes of others. Before, you may have wanted to damage their reputation out of spite, but now you want to boost it out of love.

19

How Do I Help My Bitter Spouse or Friend?

Maybe this is not your besetting sin, but you know and love someone who is entangled in it. What can you do? What if they don't see it or admit it?

A HUSBAND'S VIEW OF HIS BITTER WIFE

I asked Dave to write about his attempts to convince me of reality:

> Christians love the expression, "Speak the truth in love," but I caution you to tread very carefully when confronting someone about their bitterness. I imagine this is even truer for a husband confronting his wife, since women are so driven by emotion. To dismiss her perception as an absurd distortion will not win her confidence, nor will it help her. If you want to gain her trust, you must step carefully through your conversa-

tions when she is overwhelmed by inaccurate perceptions.

I suspect that everyone who first encounters a bitter person responds with "truth":

> *Bitter person—* *"My parents hate me."*
> *Friend—* *"Don't be ridiculous! Of course they love you very much."*

"Logical" responses to "ridiculous" statements flow very easily, but they are counterproductive in the beginning stages. What your spouse (or friend) needs at that moment is not to be hit over the head with an obvious truth but to feel empathy from the one person she feels is on her side. I wasn't very good at this for about twenty years. I live in a logical world. I am confident in my ability to persuade people, so Linda's crazy notions were simply a challenge for me to solve with persuasive logic. Ha! The joke was on me. All I accomplished with my eloquent arguments was distancing myself from her as she felt even more isolated and alone in a world of people who really didn't like her (or so she thought).

I wasn't the only one that seemingly failed her, though. There were others who were high on Linda's "hit list" of offenders. Many people managed to move on and off that list, but a couple who had their names etched in granite alongside mine were her boss (our pastor) and her parents. The beauty of that was, if one of them committed an offense, I came off as being more loving by comparison, as long as I listened and showed sympathy. Even though I got a bit of a respite from Linda's ire, she was miserable most of the time. There were very few moments when there was no one for her to be upset with. Her life was one of emotional pain, and there were constant reminders that haunted her even in times of relative quietness and solitude.

It's very painful for me to read his words. It's an ugly picture. But the truth is that the family and friends of a bitter person are suffering also.

FAITHFUL FRIENDS

Since the main object of my bitterness was the pastor of our church, I couldn't discuss it with very many people. I did vent my frustration and anger to a couple of out-of-state friends who don't know Doug. They assumed I was painting an accurate picture of him and our situation. They were sympathetic to me, which is what I wanted. What if they had known to listen for signs of bitterness and questioned me about it? Would it have helped? I don't know. It might have. I do know that God did eventually use the hard but loving words of a friend to get my attention.

As I mentioned earlier, Bob (my elder) kindly told me I was bitter. Why did I listen to him and not others? Because he and his wife took the time to hear me out, and I believed that they cared. We went out for dinner a couple of times where I ranted about Doug and his awful, unfair treatment of me.

They listened. They didn't say much, really. They certainly didn't agree with my conclusion that Doug was a monster. (They know and love him dearly.) But they also did not condemn me. They were sympathetic to the pain and turmoil I was experiencing. Once in a while, they would make gentle statements like, "You may be misjudging him there," or "That's kind of unfair." But they also said things like, "Maybe that wasn't the best thing Doug could have said, but we are all in a process, and we need to show each other grace along the way." I thought, "Maybe I don't show him much grace. Hmm."

I believe the key words in dealing with a bitter person are *gentleness, compassion,* and *love.* Even when they finally did say, "You are bitter," they said it in a gentle and caring way. I didn't feel attacked, I felt cared for. My first response to that was, "Maybe I am. I probably am. But what does that mean?"

If they had reacted initially by saying, "Shame on you, Linda! Don't you know better? This is slander. You shouldn't talk about our pastor this way. You are harboring bitterness and need to repent!" I would have been long gone by now (remember, a bitter person is often deeply wounded). I would be somewhere else, probably still trapped in my bitterness and making other peoples' lives miserable. And let me point out here, they could have said all that. It would have been entirely accurate and absolutely true. But it would not have encouraged me toward repentance. How thankful I am for their wisdom and care for me.

But showing concern and gentleness to the bitter party is

only part of this process. Only God can break through and convict a bitter person of their sin. We must pray fervently for those who are trapped in this web because only the Holy Spirit can heal their wounds and change their minds. We can hold them accountable and encourage them, but we cannot change them. We must pray that God will do His work and leave it in His hands.

Another (happy!) page from my story:

When my husband has time to sit and enjoy sporting events or a movie on TV, he sometimes falls asleep on the sofa. I used to interpret it as a personal rejection. It was supposed to be something we were doing *together.* So if I turned to him with a comment or question, and found him asleep, I would conclude, "Obviously he doesn't care if I'm here or not." We would argue, and he would explain that he enjoys dozing off. He feels warm and comfortable. It's his way of enjoying the experience. It is not anything against me, and he certainly doesn't mean to imply rejection.

I couldn't understand or accept that, so I reacted very unkindly to him at first—waking him abruptly or yelling that he was missing the big play. After a while, I just quit watching with him. Why invite blatant rejection from the one who's supposed to love me? After the Lord started showing me my sin, I realized this was bitterness against my husband. The Lord graciously changed my attitude. I now feel happy and content when my husband is snoozing in front of the football game. I don't resent him for it. I see the entire situation in a different light. I would never have believed that my heart and attitude could change so drastically if I hadn't personally experienced it.

PART IV

The Bitter End

.

20

The End of My Story

HAS LINDA CHANGED?

The following is how her husband David answered that question.

"Changed" doesn't cut it. Linda has been transformed.

At the height of her battle, Linda's life was one of deep emotional anguish. Her primary way of coping was to escape by pouring herself into books (most of little intellectual value) and other mind-numbing pursuits. She would devote hours and even days to these things because this was the only way to turn her mind off to the "realities" that plagued her: the thought that no one loved her, the idea that her boss could barely tolerate her, that her parents had no interest in her, that her husband disapproved of everything she did, and on and on. Most damaging was the constant perception that God disapproved of her. How could He possibly love her?

Linda's demeanor was usually gloomy. The glass wasn't just half-empty – it was bone dry. She would lash out in anger over the smallest of offenses. Her life was one of impossible expectations. She would predetermine exactly how an anticipated exchange with someone should play out to make her happy, and if things didn't go according to her un-communicated plan, it would confirm her "realities." She effectively squashed my sense of worth as a husband, often failed to demonstrate the deep love she has for our children, routinely lashed out with harsh words at worship team members and others, and made Doug's life miserable.

Linda would recite years' worth of events and conversations to fan the flames of her bitterness, but rarely without some sort of imagined twist. Slightly changing the words or even inflection of a conversation was all that was needed to back up her heartfelt convictions about that person's disdain for her. She didn't intentionally misrepresent these conversations. Rather, she was so convinced of how the other person felt about her that she would "hear" words that were never said and miss those that were. She was, for all intents and purposes, "hearing-impaired." I could say, "You look beautiful today," and ten minutes later she could, with full sincerity, complain that I never tell her that I find her attractive.

Throughout all of this, she maintained a faint flame of desire to please God and would try to put on a good face in public, yet the true face of a bitter woman was always just below the surface. Life was miserable for both of us.

But the Lord honored that faint flame. The Holy Spirit began a work in her that is nothing short of miraculous, and that refining work continues to this day. It started very simply as she began to recognize some of her reactions as bitterness. The transformation came, though, only as she submitted to the Holy Spirit's prompting to repent of her sin. The focus shifted dramatically from her wanting everyone else to change their behavior to a disciplined approach of confessing and owning up to her own sin each time bitterness reared its ugly head. This was true even on the rare occasions that someone truly wronged her.

What a difference repentance makes! As the heavy burden that she had been carrying around for decades began to lift, I saw genuine peace and happiness begin to flood into her life. There has been a softening of her heart that has made her a joy to live with. I no longer "walk on eggshells" around her. There is rarely any tension in our household. I watched as the mother of our two wonderful children became much more expressive of her deep love for them and extended grace when they would say or do things that, in the past, would have evoked over-the-top reactions. I had the privilege of sitting with her as she related her story to her parents, took ownership of the sin in her life, expressed her love for them, and asked for forgiveness. I've watched as she's learned how to rightly interpret the words of her pastor, boss, and friend, Doug, and to extend grace in those occasional instances when he could have said or done something better. And I've experienced love and forgiveness from the one I love with all of my heart. I'm far from a perfect husband. In fact, I can be quite insensitive, critical, and un-affirming. But Linda doesn't hold these things against me any longer. Does she think I could be a better husband? Of course – because I should be. But she no longer clings to every wrong that I've ever done to her –

she can't even recount many past offenses anymore – and she extends more grace than I deserve.

Most of all, I see a woman through whom I believe God is going to do an incredible work within His church. Having gone through this experience, we both understand why bitterness is listed in the Bible with some pretty heavy-duty sins. We are convinced that it may be one of the most prevalent sins within the modern-day church. Linda **What a difference repentance makes!** is uniquely qualified to proclaim to whoever will listen that the Holy Spirit is powerful enough to free people from the death-spiral of bitterness. This journey with Linda was one full of heartache, but I wouldn't trade one moment of it if God will use her to help others repent of their bitterness. I now see the beauty of Christ being lived out in front of me in Linda's life, and I look forward with great anticipation to how He will use her to minister to others. All glory be to God!

IS THERE REALLY A DIFFERENCE?

The following is how Doug answered that question.

I have had a front row seat for this remarkable story of God's powerful grace. Actually, I am not so much a spectator as part of the supporting cast. So I can tell you firsthand that what you read in this book is true and truly amazing.

I have known Linda since 1999. We have been friends some of that time. For the rest, it was more like enemies. No, that's not quite right. Maybe *frenemy* is the term. We have served the Lord Jesus together. We have led worship together. We have persevered through tragedy together. She was a tremendous blessing and encouragement during my greatest personal trial. And yet, there were days when I was convinced that she hated me. That a relationship like ours could exist would have been hard for me to believe if not for the fact that I was neck deep in the middle of it.

As difficult as it was at times, I wouldn't change a thing. I have never experienced such a clear and powerful display of God's sanctifying work. Linda's story gives me hope for all of the people I counsel who seem defeated by their sin. I believe like never before that people can be changed. Regardless of how deeply rooted your struggles or how persistent your temptations, the Holy Spirit *can* bring transformation. Jesus is still sanctifying His bride. There is hope for your pursuit of righteousness and for others whose sinful thorns regularly stick in your skin.

I should clarify something at this point. Our strife was not all Linda's fault. Looking back, I see many ways that I could have treated her with more love and grace. I see my own pride and selfishness. But that's just the thing about bitterness (which, hopefully, you have learned), it doesn't need anything outside of itself to flourish. Even if I had shown greater patience and care (which I wish I had done), we probably would have ended up in the same pit. But, of course, that is precisely where God's grace proves to be the most gracious. So I say, take courage! God did not leave Linda there, and He can bring a similar rescue to your situation.

If you are tempted to anger, even on a small scale, please let Linda's story help you. Learn from her. Listen to her advice.

Look at yourself honestly and take the steps necessary to overcome those temptations. It's part of walking worthy of Christ. It is also the path to joy for your friends and family. And if you are close to someone steeped in bitterness, your task is two-fold: First, you must consistently show Christ-like grace, kindness, and forbearance. It truly is a matter of dying to self for the benefit of someone you love. Second, you must pray. Really pray. Pray like Jesus in Gethsemane, like David for Bathsheba's son, like the persistent widow. Pray specifically and earnestly. Pray until you move the mighty and tender hand of your heavenly Father. Then pray more.

I encourage you to read this book again and again. And give a copy to someone else who may need to read it. If they will let her, Linda will show them the path to freedom in Christ, no matter how strong the chains feel right now.

Finally, I want to say how much joy it brings me to say that Linda is my friend. It took great courage for her to reveal, with brutal honesty, the ugliness of sin and the beauty of redemption. But I'm not surprised that she did it because she is different. She is truly humble and vulnerable. She admits her failures and how far there is yet to go. But above all, she speaks of the glory of God's amazing grace, which is the only explanation for the affection we now share.

A FINAL WORD FROM LINDA

Actually, my story has not ended. I still fight the temptations to bitterness. Last month was a struggle – last weekend was a temptation. I am sure this will be an ongoing battle for me, but it is so much easier than it used to be. Praise God!

Yesterday my feelings were hurt. The Lord helped me to cover it with love. Last weekend I was thinking, "Poor me. I'm so tired. No one cares," and I realized I was indulging in self-pity. Did I stop immediately? No, but much sooner than I would have previously. If I had allowed it to continue, I may have found myself blaming someone (my friend, my husband, my pastor) for the way I was feeling. Then I might have thought up instances from the past where they failed me or I was disappointed in them and *Bam!* I could have slid into full-fledged bitterness just like that! It is an easy trip for me, so I must be careful. I went to the Lord with my struggle, after some firm self-talk, and asked for His forgiveness and help.

I am also increasingly aware of this temptation or tendency in others. I have a heightened "bitterness radar" and an increased burden for those who fall prey to this insidious sin. If this is your area of struggle, please don't gloss over it or fail to take it seriously. No sin is unimportant, but I believe this one is particularly easy to justify or ignore.

However, I praise God! He has worked in me. I am not the same person I was. Today, something may shake me for a few hours or a few days, but with the Lord's strength I fight through it. I ask the Lord to show me what I'm thinking and what dangerous territory I may be entering, and He does.

My marriage is better than ever. (My husband has already told you about the radical change he sees.) I have a warm friendship and work relationship with Doug. I have worked hard to repent of my sin toward my parents, to forgive their sins against me, and to take steps to love and bless them. I have asked the Lord to give me wisdom and love, and He has answered.

My desire is to be the woman described in Proverbs:

> *She is clothed with strength and dignity;*
> *she can laugh at the days to come.*
> *She speaks with wisdom,*
> *and faithful instruction is on her tongue.*
> *(Proverbs 31:25-26 NIV)*

Finally, the apostle Paul says, "And they praised God because of me" (Galatians 1:24 NIV). May this be true in my case as well.

All glory to Jesus!

PART V

Appendix

21

Review: What I'd Like You to Come Away With in Twelve Points

Here, in list form, are the key points I have tried to make through all the discussion and examples of the previous chapters. Use them as quick reminders of the bitter truth.

1. Bitterness is sin. It is deceitful because it is a response to an offense done to you, making it easy to excuse your reaction or blame the offender.

2. The main pathways leading to bitterness are anger, self-pity, and unmet expectations.

3. The primary way you will act out this sin is through your words.

4. Bitterness is called a root in Scripture because it affects others and gets entangled with other sins.

5. A bitter person is angry, unkind, unhappy, and biased in their thinking.

6. Bitterness crowds out spiritual growth in one's life and sets him or her at odds with God and others.

7. Bitterness becomes a habit, an ingrained way of thinking.

8. Active, unselfish, persevering love is the remedy for bitterness.

9. We must realize that our bitterness is sin, repent of it, then forgive and love others.

10. God will forgive your sin and free you of bitterness when you ask. *He* gives you power to repent and to forgive others.

11. You should respond to calamities by submitting to and worshipping God.

12. You should respond to wrongs done to you by:

- Recognizing and submitting to God's sovereignty. Your suffering is part of His wise plan for you.

- Asking God to increase your love so you can cover their sins with it.

- Confronting if necessary, but always and only in love.

- Forgive, forgive, forgive. Ask God to give you a forgiving heart. He promises He will.

22

Contact Me

I would love to encourage you if you are struggling with bitterness or hear how the Lord helped you overcome. Please tell me your story. You can reach me at www.bittertruthbook.com.

Other Books by Cross to Crown Ministries

Exalted: Putting Jesus in His Place by Douglas Goodin
God's Design for Marriage by Douglas Goodin
Woman of Grace by Anne Brown

CROSS to CROWN
M I N I S T R I E S

www.crosstocrown.org

Made in the USA
San Bernardino, CA
14 October 2014